"I used Bill Eddy to deal .... ?l
situation. I implemented his adv.... .... . s,
frustrating conflict and confrontation, I adopted an entirely
different approach, with excellent results. Bill gave me a pathway
when I thought all roads were blocked."
— Dan Solin, author of the *Smartest* series of books

"By their very nature, some people are as difficult to under-
stand as they are to work with or live with. Drawing on years of
experience with some of the most challenging personalities, Bill
Eddy offers the reader simple, practical, tools to effectively defuse
any high-conflict situation. *Biff* is a must-read."
— George Simon, Ph.D., bestselling author of
In Sheep's Clothing, Character Disturbance, and *The
Judas Syndrome*

"Bill Eddy is a master creator of simple-to-use tools for
managing and de-escalating high conflict behaviors in the
workplace. I recommend to each of my professional clients to
Bookmark or Favorite the High Conflict Institute website as
a useful "go to" resource for everyday insights and to order the
books, "It's All Your Fault" and "BIFF: Quick Responses to
High Conflict People". Bill writes with compassion to bring
greater ease to a variety of complex and difficult workplace relationships which often consume time, productivity and resources
unless managed effectively. With the many practical examples,
case scenarios and practice exercises, Bill's books are an invaluable
resource to highlight, reference regularly and share with colleagues to keep workplace dynamics in check while establishing
healthier, engaging and productive systems within the organiza-
tional culture."
— Marcia Haber, President and CEO
Discover Conflict Solutions, Inc.

"*Sometimes the most powerful interventions are the most simple.*

The most difficult skill for post-separated families to master, in my opinion, is effective communication. Typically, emotional baggage and unhelpful patterns that often were a prominent factor in the relationship breakdown, continue to undermine co-parenting long after the divouce dust has settled.

Interestingly, these same people are able to manage effective, polite and succinct communication and negotiations with others; just not their ex! Teaching them the B.I.F.F. principals (Brief, Informative, Friendly, Firm) allows them to create distance between the issues at hand and the problems of the past.

B.I.F.F. is an effective communications micro-skill that can be easily taught to all clients ranging from the extreme High Conflict Personalities (HCPs) to highly functioning individuals."

— Maria Buglar, Psychologist, Brisbane, Australia

BIFF

Quick Responses to
High-Conflict People,
Their Personal Attacks, Hostile Email,
and Social Media Meltdowns

SECOND EDITION

Bill Eddy, LCSW, Esq.
Attorney, Mediator and Therapist

UNHOOKED BOOKS
an imprint of High Conflict Institute Press
Scottsdale, Arizona

This second edition published in 2014 was first published in 2011.

Copyright © 2011 by Bill Eddy
Unhooked Books, LLC
7701 E. Indian School Rd., Ste. F
Scottsdale, AZ 85251
www.unhookedbooks.com

Cover design by Gordan Blazevik
Book Interior design by KarrieRoss.com
Edited by Anne Terashima

Library of Congress Cataloging-in-Publication Data

Eddy, William A.
   BIFF : Quick Responses to High-Conflict People, Their Personal Attacks, Hostile Email and Social Media Meltdowns / Bill Eddy. -- [Second edition].
      pages cm
      ISBN 978-1-936268-72-6 (paperback) -- ISBN 978-1-936268-79-5 (ebook)
   1. Conflict management. 2. Interpersonal conflict. 3. Social media I. Title.
   HM1126.E33 2014
   303.6'9--dc23
                          2014014444
            Printed in the United States of America.

It's All Your Fault at Work! Managing Narcissists and Other High-Conflict People

So, What's Your Proposal? Shifting High-Conflict People from Blaming to Problem-Solving in 30 Seconds

New Ways for Work: Personal Skills for Productive Relationships
Coaching Manual
Workbook

It's All Your Fault! 12 Tips for Managing People Who Blame Others for Everything

High Conflict People in Legal Disputes

Managing High Conflict People in Court

New Ways for Mediation: More Skills, More Structure and Less Stress
Seminar & Demonstration (DVD)

Don't Alienate the Kids! Raising Resilient Children While Avoiding High Conflict Divorce

Splitting: Protecting Yourself While Divorcing Someone with Borderline or Narcissistic Personality Disorder

The Future of Family Court: Structure, Skills and Less Stress

New Ways for Families in Separation and Divorce
Professional Guidebook
Parent Workbook

Collaborative Parent Workbook
Decision Skills Class Instructor's Manual
Decision Skills Class Workbook
Pre-Mediation Coaching Manual
Pre-Mediation Coaching Workbook

Splitting America: How Politicians, Super PACs and the News Mirror High Conflict Divorce

ACKNOWLEDGEMENTS

I THANK MY WIFE, ALICE, for her continuing tolerance of my writing obsession and her willingness to give me clinical and editorial feedback. I thank Megan Hunter for all of her work in editing and managing the publication of this book, as well as her work in developing High Conflict Institute. I am appreciative of my ongoing writing collaborations with Randi Kreger, publishing advice from Scott Edelstein, and editing from Anne Terashima, which have helped in the creation of this book. The following gave me very useful and timely feedback on this book from varied perspectives: Dennis Doyle, Mariel Diaz and Austin Manghan. Many other people, including many clients and colleagues, have contributed their ideas, their experience and their encouragement to me and High Conflict Institute, but they are too many to be adequately named here – you know who you are.

CONTENTS

CHAPTER ONE

High-Conflict People and Blamespeak

Has anyone ever told you:
 "It's all YOUR fault!"
 "You should be ashamed of yourself!"
 "You're a disgrace to your _____!"
 [family][community][country][team][profession][party]
 [you fill in the blank]

 "What's the matter with you? Are you crazy? Stupid? Immoral? Unethical? Evil?"
 And then were you told everything that's "wrong" with you and how you should behave?

It's Not About You!

Let's face it. Most of us have said something like this when we "lost it" – hopefully not too often. But some people communicate this way a lot! It's helpful to know that their personal attacks are not about you. They are about the *blamer's* inability to control himself and solve problems.

When people repeatedly use personal attacks, I think of them as "high-conflict people" (HCPs), because they lack skills for dealing well with conflict. Instead of sharing responsibility for solving problems, they repeatedly lose it and *increase* conflict by making it intensely personal and taking no responsibility. They are the most difficult people, because they are preoccupied with blaming others – what I call their "targets of blame" – which may include you! They speak Blamespeak: Attack, defend – and attack again.

I wrote this book to help you respond to anyone who tries to engage you with hostile emails, texts, Facebook and other social media postings, vicious rumors or just plain difficult behavior. But before I explain how to write a BIFF response, I want to give you a brief understanding of how HCPs think. To deal with them successfully requires a shift in how *you* think about them - so that you know what *not to do*, as well as what to do. Your BIFF responses will be better if you know this. (If you want to start writing BIFF Responses right away, go straight to Chapter Two).

High-Conflict Personalities

HCPs have a repeated pattern of aggressive behavior that increases conflict rather than reducing or resolving it. It may be part of their personalities – how they automatically and unconsciously think, feel and behave – and they carry this pattern with them. They tend to have a lot of:

- **All-or-nothing thinking** (one person is all good, another is all bad)
- **Unmanaged emotions** (exaggerated anger, fear, sadness – out of proportion to events)
- **Extreme behavior** (yelling, hitting, lying, spreading rumors, impulsive actions, etc.)
- **Preoccupation with blaming others** (people close to them or people in authority)

To HCPs, it seems normal and necessary to intensely blame others. They can't restrain themselves, even though their blaming may harm themselves as well.

When problems and conflicts arise, instead of looking for solutions, HCPs look for someone to blame. They have an all-or-nothing approach. They think that it must be all *your* fault or else it might appear to be all *their* fault – and they can't cope with that possibility for psychological reasons. They become preoccupied with blaming others in order to escape being blamed themselves. But you can't point this out to them, because they become even *more* defensive.

To HCPs, conflict often feels like a life or death struggle. This explains why it may feel like they are engaged in campaigns to destroy you or someone else. They feel that their survival is at stake, so they often show unmanaged emotions and extreme behaviors – even in routine conflicts or under normal pressures.

You don't need to figure out whether someone is a high-conflict person. If you suspect someone is an HCP, just respond more carefully and understand that the person may have less self-control than you do. BIFF responses are a good method for coping with HCPs – and you can use them with anyone!

Lack of Self-Awareness

The hardest thing to "get" about HCPs is that they lack an awareness of how they contribute to their own problems. They honestly view other people as causing the way they feel and the way they act. "She makes me feel this way." "He made me do it." They think they *have to* react the way they do, in order to protect themselves or to connect with people without feeling extremely vulnerable psychologically. They may be aware that other people react negatively to them, but they think that it's everyone else's fault.

Sure, they may be aware that they are lying sometimes or manipulating sometimes. But they feel that they *have to* lie and manipulate, because of unmanaged fears within themselves that they are not aware of. And you can't tell them that! And you can't change them! Trying to point out these hidden feelings will most likely trigger an intense rage against you. They're hidden for a reason.

For many HCPs, this pattern of behavior is the result of childhood abuse. They learned that it didn't matter whether they were bad or good – they still got physically hit, verbally abused, ignored, neglected or otherwise abused. They grew up learning that aggressive behavior is how you solve problems.

For other HCPs, it is a result of being raised with a strong sense of entitlement and exaggerated self-esteem. They learned that it didn't matter whether they were good or bad – they still got what they wanted! This seems to have increased in society since the 1970's with the increased emphasis on self-esteem. While having low self-esteem is a bad thing, too much self-esteem is also a bad thing – if it teaches people that they are superior to others and that they can get whatever they want, without learning skills and without working for it.

In both cases, abuse or entitlement, HCPs have not learned that their own behavior creates or worsens the conflict situations they are in. In many ways, this is a disability, as HCPs can't see the connection between their own actions and how others respond to them. They don't know how to solve relationship problems, so they make things worse and don't understand why they feel so miserable so much of the time. They turn these feelings into blaming others – and staying upset. Because blaming others doesn't solve problems.

Lack of Self-Change

Since they lack self-awareness, HCPs make no effort to change their own behavior when things go badly. They view complex problems and relationships as all another person's responsibility and don't see their own part in causing the problem or finding a solution. They don't change their own behavior to try to make things better, so things don't get better. In fact, they are highly defensive about their own behavior, so they put all of their energy into defending their own actions and shifting the blame to others. Finding easy ways to avoid unnecessarily triggering this "HCP defensiveness" will make your life a lot easier.

Ordinary people are constantly changing their own behavior. They want to be more successful in their lives and they learn from their experience and their mistakes. But HCPs don't seem to learn from their social mistakes – even when you try to make them see it. Forget about it!

Don't say: "Look in the mirror, Buddy!" You'll just make things worse.

That's why BIFF responses seem to work so well. They don't trigger HCP defensiveness when done correctly. The goal is to disengage from the HCP's blaming behavior. It's not easy. It takes practice to change your own behavior while dealing with an HCP's behavior. But by changing your own behavior, you can change the interaction and relationship dynamics. You can do it if you are a reasonable person who is self-aware and continues to learn and change. I wrote this book for you.

Personality Disorders

HCPs appear to have traits associated with personality disorders, which include lack of self-awareness and lack of self-change. Personality disorders are a mental health diagnosis for problems that are part of someone's personality, including seriously dysfunctional ways of thinking, handling their emotions, and behaving. People with these disorders are stuck in a narrow range of repeated behavior that prevents them from having satisfying relationships and keeps them highly distressed. Yet they are not aware of their own patterns and don't try to change them. They tend to believe that their problems are caused by someone or something else.

Mental health professionals have been treating personality disorders for many decades and have identified several different types. However, only qualified mental health professionals can diagnose a personality disorder in someone, after careful consideration of many factors. One of the characteristics of a personality disorder is that people with such a disorder don't recognize that they have it, because they lack self-awareness.

People around such a person often recognize that he or she has some kind of mental health problem, but it seems to come and go. People with personality disorders often do well some of the time, such as in school or in a job, but have a hard time in close relationships or dealing with people in authority positions. It's often not obvious until you get close to the person and there is a conflict or a crisis.

Personality Disorders Appear to be Increasing

Recent research suggests that more and more people are growing up with personality disorders. This may explain why there appears to be an increase in the number of high-conflict people. A recent study done by the National Institutes of Health between 2001 and 2005 suggests an increasing trend in the percentage of people who meet the criteria for a personality disorder. The researchers interviewed over 35,000 people, who were considered representative of the United States' population. They analyzed the results by four age groups. The following are the study results for the five personality disorders which I believe are most often associated with high-conflict behavior:

Narcissistic = **6.2% of US population**
(62% male; 38% female)
Common conflict traits: arrogance, superiority, lack of empathy, insulting, self-centered

By age group:
65+ = **3.2%**   64-45 = **5.6%**   44-30 = **7.1%**   29-20 yrs. = **9.4%**

Borderline = **5.9% of US population**
(47% male; 53% female)
Common conflict traits: sudden intense anger, wide mood swings, revenge and vindication

By age group:
65+ = **2.0%**   64-45 = **5.5%**   44-30 = **7.0%**   29-20 yrs. = **9.3%**

Paranoid = **4.4% of US population**
(43% male; 57% female)
Common traits extreme fearfulness, mistrusts everyone, fears conspiracies and betrayals

By age group:
65+ = **1.8%**   64-45 = **3.6%**   44-30 = **5.0%**   29-18 yrs. = **6.8%**

Antisocial = **3.6% of US population**
(74% male; 26% female)
Common traits: criminality, lying, fearless, enjoys bullying/ hurting others, likes to dominate

By age group:
65+ = **0.6%**   64-45 = **2.8%**   44-30 = **4.2%**   29-18 yrs. = **6.2%**

Histrionic = **1.8% of US population**
(51% male; 49% female)
Common traits: excessive drama, highly emotional, exaggerates, demands attention, may lie

By age group:
65+ = **0.6%**   64-45 = **1.2%**   44-30 = **1.8%**   29-18 yrs. = **3.8%**

There is a lot of overlap, so that many people who fit in one category may have two or more personality disorders. Also, the researchers found that there was a lot of overlap with other mental disorders, such as depression, anxiety, bipolar disorder, substance abuse and addiction, suicidal thoughts and actual suicides.

Each of these personality disorders has a list of symptoms or "maladaptive personality traits," which mental health professionals look for in determining whether someone can be diagnosed as having a personality disorder. Many people have some of these traits, but not enough for a personality disorder. Keep in mind that only qualified mental health professionals can diagnose a personality disorder, and just a few traits is not considered a disorder at all. Also, children under eighteen are usually not considered to have personality disorders, because they are changing so rapidly and often show extreme emotions and behaviors while they are learning to become more balanced and mature.

While the data above made the researchers wonder if these personality disorders may fade with time, they admit they have no evidence supporting that theory. In general, personalities don't change much over a person's lifetime, unless they work hard at making changes. People with personality disorders usually don't try to change, because they can't see that they have a problem. They think that problems are always someone else's fault.

My theory is that personality disorders are increasing in modern society and that each future generation will have even more personality disorders and, therefore, more high-conflict people, if current trends continue. As our society increasingly teaches violence, extreme emotions and extreme behaviors in movies, on television, over the Internet, and in the news, these tendencies will become absorbed into personality development for some children as they grow up. Fortunately, the percentages are still small, but they seem to be increasing rapidly. This means that the need (and opportunity) for writing BIFF responses will grow more and more important over the years.

HCPs and Personality Disorders

Not all people with personality disorders are HCPs, because many of those with personality disorders are not preoccupied with targets of blame. They are just stuck in a narrow pattern of dysfunctional behavior.

And not all HCPs have a personality disorder. Many HCPs just have some difficult personality traits, but not a disorder at all. I want to emphasize that being a high-conflict person does not mean someone has a mental disorder. HCP is not a diagnosis – it's a descriptive term for someone who has a lot of high-conflict behavior in relationships.

So don't tell someone you think that she has a personality disorder! And don't tell someone you think that he is a high-conflict person. Their HCP defensiveness may make your life miserable for months or years to come. And you may be wrong!

Instead, I recommend that you have a *private working theory* that someone may be an HCP. You don't tell the person and you don't assume you are right. It really doesn't matter! You simply focus on key methods to help in *managing* your relationship, whether or not you are dealing with an HCP. Use your *private working theory* to change your own behavior, not theirs.

While a BIFF response itself isn't going to change anyone, it should help you end a conversation that has been escalating out of control.

For more information about personality disorders and managing high-conflict people in general, see my book *It's All YOUR Fault! 12 Tips for Managing People Who Blame Others for Everything* (2008, HCI Press).

For dealing with a high-conflict divorce, see *Splitting: Protecting Yourself While Divorcing Someone with Borderline or Narcissistic Personality Disorder* by Eddy and Kreger (2011, New Harbinger Press).

Blamespeak

Blamespeak is the term I use for the language of high-conflict blaming. It has increased rapidly over the past ten years, although it's been around for eternity. While everyone may "lose" it and use Blamespeak on rare occasions, HCPs use it a lot.

Blamespeak often sounds like the intimate, disrespectful way that young children talk to their siblings or their parents in anger in the privacy of their homes before they learn how to be adults with adult self-restraint: "I hate you!" "You're an idiot!" "I'm never speaking to you again!" Then a minute later, these young children are playing happily together. Unfortunately, such intimate disrespect has broken out into the airwaves and onto the screens, with modern radio, TV, movies and the Internet. And there's no playing together afterwards.

It is a way of interacting with others that avoids the vulnerability of true adult relationships. It may be a result of never learning the self-restraint skills that children used to learn in their families and communities. Blamespeak would be considered child-like behavior, except that it is demonstrated today by some of the most powerful people in our society. It is a way of getting attention at a time of rapid change, when there are fewer established ways of getting attention – such as used to occur within a large family, a tight community, or stable religious and political organizations.

If you want attention these days, you have to grab it! And Blamespeak is the cheapest and easiest way to grab attention in our society. Our brains are wired to pay the most attention to emergencies – following the nonverbal cues of extreme facial expressions, tone of voice and hand gestures. This is what you see on our screens today. Blamespeak does grab your attention!

Unfortunately, electronic media has the ability to manipulate our emergency brain wiring, by repeating the exact same blaming words and tone of voice over and over and over again. This gives these repeated words exaggerated power and respect, which hijacks our attention and makes us believe we *are* in danger and *should be* more anxious than circumstances truly warrant. Have you noticed how hard it is to ignore loud, dramatic and intense Blamespeak in the news and on your own computer screen – every day?

Recognizing Blamespeak

You can recognize Blamespeak by the following characteristics, which make it hard to ignore:

1. It's usually **emotionally intense** and out of proportion to the issues. Sometimes it can seem calm, but be subtle and passive aggressive and bring out the worst

in a reasonable person's response. Blamespeak is never boring.

2. It's **very personal**: about your intelligence, sanity, memory, ethics, sex life, looks, etc.

3. It's **all your fault**: the Blamespeaker feels no responsibility for the problem or the solution.

4. It's **out of context**: it ignores all of the good you've done and all of the bad the Blamespeaker has done.

5. It's often **shared with others** to emphasize how "blame*worthy*" you are and how "blame*less*" the speaker is. The Blamespeaker has no sense of shame, embarrassment, or boundaries. He or she will speak this way about you in public. Unfortunately, Blamespeak often sounds believable to those who aren't informed about your situation.

6. You have an **intensely negative gut feeling** about the Blamespeak, which sickens you, makes you feel fearful, suddenly helpless, and/or very angry at someone: the Blamespeaker or another one of their targets of blame.

7. You find yourself **compelled to respond with Blamespeak** of your own. It is extremely hard to step back to prepare a reasonable response, or to decide not to respond at all.

Responding to Blamespeak

Many people initially react to Blamespeak with Blamespeak of their own ("counter Blamespeak") – even people who are not ordinarily high-conflict people. Such counter attacks are a normal human response to the unrestrained aggressive behavior of others. Your counter attack might even be true. But pointing it out to an HCP won't change anything. Usually it will just escalate the situation. For example, you might be tempted to say or write:

> YOU'RE the one who's stupid, crazy and unethical! Let me tell you what's really...
>
> Look in the mirror, Buddy! Here's what you'll see...
>
> You're an idiot if you think I'm going to respond to your long-winded B.S. and incoherent babbling (or lies)!
>
> If you don't do something about this problem, I'm going to expose your illegal, fraudulent and unethical behavior to everyone! First of all, ...
>
> You have no clue what you are talking about and should just shut up! I'll tell you ...

Such counter Blamespeak not only doesn't work, it also makes you look like an HCP to those outside the situation. Then, the HCP uses your reaction to justify a new round of Blamespeak, and on and on. The key is to not over-react, but to respond quickly with a BIFF response to Blamespeak. Or not to respond at all, which is often the best idea.

The rest of this book gives you a simple strategy for knowing when and how to respond to Blamespeak – or any frustrating behavior – with a BIFF response. Chapters Four through Nine provide BIFF responses to specific situations, but they also add tips which you may find helpful in any setting. Chapters Three and Ten explain some recent brain research that indicates that *you* may influence how others will respond to you, by how you choose to respond to them. So choose your words carefully.

CHAPTER TWO

Writing a BIFF Response

BIFF responses (or "BIFFs") are usually in writing, although they can be in person as well. BIFF stands for:

BRIEF

INFORMATIVE

FRIENDLY

FIRM

This may seem easy, but it's actually pretty hard to do at first – while restraining yourself from doing Blamespeak back. It's often helpful to step back and not respond right away. Here's a short description of each step:

BRIEF

Your response should be very short: one paragraph of 2-5 sentences in most cases. It doesn't matter how long the Blamespeak statement that you are responding to is. The point is to avoid triggering HCP defensiveness in the other person and focusing them on problem-solving information. Don't give too many words for the other person to react to. The more you say, the more likely you are to trigger another

Blamespeak response – which doesn't do you
any good.

Keeping it brief isn't easy. When I can, I give
my BIFF responses to someone else to review
before I send them out. The reviewer almost
always cuts them down – often in half.

INFORMATIVE

Give a sentence or two of straight, useful
information on the subject being discussed.
If there isn't a real subject or issue (because the
personality is the issue), you can still give some
related helpful information. It shifts the discussion to an objective subject, rather than opinions
about each other. Don't include your opinion or
defensiveness about the subject. Just provide
straight information, presented in neutral terms,
as briefly as possible.

FRIENDLY

This is often the hardest part, but very important. You can start out by saying something like:
"Thank you for telling me your opinion on this
subject." Or: "I appreciate your concerns."
Or just: "Thanks for your email. Let me give you
some information you may not have…" You can
also end it with a friendly comment. For example: "I hope you have a nice weekend."

FIRM

The goal of many BIFF responses is to end the
conversation – to disengage from a potentially
high-conflict situation. You want to let the other

person know that this is really all you are going to say on the subject. In some cases, you will give two clear choices for future action. If you need a response, then it often helps to set a firm reply date. If you are going to take action if the other person does not do something, then you could say, for example: "If I don't receive the information I need by such and such date, then I will have to do such and such. I really hope that won't be necessary." (Note that this is both firm and friendly.)

It's Not What You Feel Like Doing

Of course, BIFF responses are often not what you feel like doing. You may hate each of the steps I described above. You may feel more like strangling the other person – or getting out of town. That's because Blamespeak is a lot more fun and feels much stronger. It is self-satisfying.

But the reality is that Blamespeak gives you about a twenty-minute high, much like cocaine or some other drug. Then it vanishes when the other person responds with more Blamespeak and you get that sickening, fearful or angry feeling inside again. Or the other person will share your Blamespeak with people important to you and you will have to explain yourself to them.

BIFF responses don't usually give you a high. But they can give you a sense of relief, can end a high-conflict discussion and may even solve a problem.

Do You Need to Respond?

In many cases, it's better not to respond at all. Here are some Blamespeak situations you can ignore:

> - When no one else is involved in the communication except you and the other person.
> - When there is clearly no real issue being discussed (their personality is the issue).
> - When it is simply the other person's opinion about your behavior, personality, etc.
> - When it is clear that you will not change the other person's point of view.
> - When you have already responded sufficiently on the same subject.

When to Respond with a BIFF

In general, it's best to respond quickly, after having your response reviewed by someone else (if possible), for three reasons:

- HCPs tend to believe that you agree with their opinions of you unless you quickly disagree. Unfortunately, silence means consent in their defensive ways of thinking.
- HCPs often tell other people about all the bad things that you have "done" in their minds. If other people

don't hear that you disagree, then the HCP's comments are assumed to be true by the other people.

- HCPs' Blamespeak is so extremely blaming and emotionally intense that their statements sound and feel true – even when they are not. (Emotions are contagious and *intense* emotions are *intensely* contagious.) So their *emotions* often persuade others that you are acting very badly and that the HCP is a victim, unless you can quickly inform them with factual information that distracts and counters the emotions.

For example:

HCP: "He never responded to my request. I was left hanging for weeks and it cost me a lot."

This statement isn't true because you did respond. But it sounds true – and influences the listener's opinion of you. If you don't respond quickly, it becomes a given fact and opinions become established about you and your organization.

Many people in positions of authority, including businesses, government agencies and politicians, often make the mistake of assuming that people will not take Blamespeak seriously, so they don't respond or wait much too long. It's easy to find examples of this on a regular basis in the news.

HCP: "She never lets me spend time with my daughter."

This statement isn't true, but it sounds true. In close relationships (or previously close relationships), you're a jerk until proven innocent. If you don't respond, it must mean it's true.

To Whom Should You Respond?

Generally, I recommend that you respond to the same person or people in the same format used by the Blamespeaker(s). If it was an email or letter from her to you, then you can respond to her by email – if at all. If it was copied to another person (friend, boss, lawyer, etc.), then you should include that person in your response. If it was sent to a group of people, then respond to the group – such as using Reply All with an email.

If the Blamespeak was made to the public, such as in the newspaper, radio or television, then you should try to reach the same audience. It's not always possible to reach the same audience with the same impact as the Blamespeak, but you should try the best you can – as quickly (and carefully) as possible. When you respond in public, it is particularly important to have it reviewed by someone else first!

What is your Goal?

There are usually three goals to consider with HCPs:

1. **To manage the relationship,** such as when you work with the person, when this person is your daughter, etc. In other words, when the relationship is important to you OR you have no way to get out of it.

2. **To reduce the relationship** to a less intense level, such as with a friend, neighbor, or even a family member.

3. **To end the relationship**, usually by phasing the person slowly out of your life.

How you respond will make a big difference to the HCP. If you inadvertently give him negative feedback, you will increase the intensity of his interactions with you, as HCPs can't handle negative feedback. It's better to use BIFFs and avoid talking about the past. Even if you are in a committed relationship or a position of authority and explaining your concerns about the past is necessary, it helps to put the emphasis on the *desired future behavior* – although you may have to acknowledge the past or address it officially. Just keep the focus on the future as much as possible.

If you are too rejecting, such as attempting to suddenly end the relationship, the HCP will increase her interactions with you and the intensity of her emotions with you – usually to try to talk you out of ending the relationship or to punish you for ending it. For this reason, I recommend "phasing out" relationships with HCPs, if you plan to end them, as they need more time to process and accept change. Otherwise, when endings are too abrupt, they may try to hold on to you by stalking you, harassing you, or suing you in an attempt to keep contact going in some manner, even if it's negative.

In many cases, people choose to reduce, but continue, their relationships with HCPs at a less intense level. This way they maintain the positive aspects – such as a shared interest – while avoiding the most negative aspects. Many employers are encouraged to take this approach, because their HCP employees are sometimes making important contributions to the organization – even though they do not have good conflict resolution skills.

Whichever goal you have, keep it in mind when interacting (or avoiding interacting) with an HCP and giving a BIFF response. Ask yourself: Will my response engage the other person more in my life? Or allow him to back off without defensiveness? Defensiveness is the key word in explaining the HCP model. Throughout the examples in this book, you will see that the main effort is to avoid triggering HCP defensiveness, while also accomplishing your goal.

A School Email Example

(Some examples are real, some are slightly altered and others are totally made up.)

Ashley: Does anybody know if we're supposed to make our own costumes for the school play? I'm not sure what we're supposed to do.

Holly: I don't know. Probably not. I think there's someone who's organizing all of that. It's on the paper somewhere. Can you believe that Brittany got the lead part?? She's so stuck up and rude to everyone. I saw her at a nice restaurant and she had no manners whatsoever. She's such a B _ _ _ _!

Sarah: Ashley, you sound like an idiot. It says NOTHING about us making our own costumes for the play. How could you make yours – you don't even know how to sew! Also, why is everyone yapping about Brittany getting the lead part. Will you NEVER stop being jealous just because she can sing?? Hello!! GET A LIFE!! And Holly - do you know anything about manners?? Has she personally offended you somehow? I mean do we really know about her manners, and intelligence? I'll answer that for you. NO!

Holly: Look at you! Do you ever READ what you write? Sarah, what do YOU know about manners! Give us a break!

Ashley: I was just trying to find out what we needed to DO! Don't worry, I'll talk to someone else. Someone with more manners than YOU!! Holly, give me a call.

But suppose that Ashley decided to use a BIFF response to Sarah's Blamespeak *instead* of what she wrote above. Would the following be a good response? Would it be a BIFF?

Ashley: Okay, Sarah. I'll ask someone else.

Is this a BIFF?

Did she consider whether she needed to respond? Suppose that she thought about it and decided that she wanted to keep Sarah as a friend. In that case, she decided to calm down the conversation and end it for now. She didn't want to ignore the conversation by not responding, because that might make Sarah think that she had "won" or intimidated her. And she didn't want to over-react with Blamespeak herself.

Brief? Yes. Very brief, but sufficient for her goal.

Informative? Yes, by saying she'll ask someone else. This way Ashley keeps the focus on her question about who is supposed to make their costumes. She lets them know she is seeking information and that's all. She totally avoids responding to everything else Sarah said.

Friendly? Somewhat. Ashley says, "Okay, Sarah." This is friendly enough, by not ignoring her or over-reacting to her, but simply acknowledging that Sarah had responded to her. She could have said, "Thanks for responding to my question." But this would have sounded sarcastic, since Sarah's response was so insulting to Ashley. When there's this much Blamespeak, it's best to just say "okay" or something similar.

Firm? Firm enough. Ashley ended the conversation. She gave Sarah nothing else to respond to.

There's no need for Ashley to tell Holly to call her. She can just call Holly herself now. No need to rub it in with Sarah that she's going to call Holly. That would just trigger Sarah's HCP defensiveness – if she is an HCP. And it doesn't matter if Sarah is an HCP or just having a bad day. A BIFF can work in both cases.

Now let's look at a family example, after a divorce. In this case, there's enough history to know that one person has a *pattern* of high-conflict behavior, so it's especially important to use a BIFF.

A Family Example

Joe's email: Jane, I can't believe you are so stupid as to think that I'm going to let you take the children to your boss' birthday party during my parenting time. Have you no memory of the last six conflicts we've had about my parenting time? Or are you having an affair with him? I always knew you would do anything to get ahead! In fact, I remember coming to your office party witnessing you making a total fool of yourself – including flirting with everyone from the CEO down to the mailroom kid! Are you high on something? Haven't you gotten your finances together enough to support yourself yet, without flinging your-self at every Tom, Dick and Harry? ... [And on and on and on for two full pages.]

Jane: Thank you for responding to my request to take the children to my office party. Just to clarify, the party will be from 3-5 on Friday at the office and there will be approximately 30 people there – including several other parents bringing school-age children. There will be no alcohol, as it is a family-oriented firm and there will be family-oriented activities. I think it will be a good experience for the kids to see me at my workplace. Since you do not agree, then of course I will respect that and withdraw my request, as I recognize it is your parenting time. [And that's the end of her email.]

Is Jane's response a BIFF?

Did she consider whether she needed to respond? Yes. Since she had made a scheduling request, she needed to let him know that she was withdrawing it. Otherwise, she could probably have ignored his email altogether. She didn't need to respond to most of what he said, so she ignored the rest.

Brief? Yes. It was just one paragraph with five sentences.

Informative? Yes. Three sentences of information about her request. They were neutral and objective, without any opinions inserted or negative comments about Joe. It included objective information, which shifts the focus from evaluating each other to evaluating details for decision-making. You will also notice that she did not spend any time countering his many allegations against her. There was no need, as she will not change his mind. It would just renew the argument. She was able to avoid getting emotionally hooked into defending herself unnecessarily.

Friendly? Yes. She said "Thank you for responding..." "Since you do not agree, then of course I will respect that..."

Firm? Yes. She ended the discussion. While she repeated her belief that it would be a good experience for the children, she did not leave it as an open question. She withdrew her request. If he changes his mind based on her information, she will be happy but she does not expect it. She is realistic and not asking him again. If she asked him again, after making her "informative" statement, she would just be opening herself up to another personal attack. So she has closed the discussion. (Of course, this doesn't prevent him from writing back and saying he changed his mind, but she knows this is highly unlikely given their history.)

Comment: Jane kept it brief, and did not engage in defending herself. Since this was just between them, she didn't even need to respond. If he sent this email to friends, co-workers or family members (which high-conflict people often do), then she would need to respond to the larger group with more information, such as the following:

Jane: Dear friends and family: As you know, Joe and I had a difficult divorce. He has sent you a private email showing correspondence between us about a parenting schedule matter. I hope you will see this as a private matter and understand that you do not need to respond or get involved in any way. Almost everything he has said is in anger and not at all accurate. If you have any questions for me personally, please feel free to contact me and I will clarify anything I can. I appreciate your friendship and support.

And that's it: BIFF. A key point here is that she didn't counter each individual allegation of Joe's. Instead, she replied that, "Almost everything he has said is in anger and not at all accurate." That takes care of it. Now everyone knows she does not agree with him. Nothing is left unchallenged. If anyone wants more information, they can contact her. Usually, family and friends are happy to stay out of it and leave them alone.

A Workplace Example

Rochelle's boss, Phil, sent an email to the manager of a major project they were working on, explaining that it was running late:

> Jim, I hope to have this project in to you by the end of the month. I know we are running about two weeks behind, so I wanted to give you the heads up now. Unfortunately, my assistant Rochelle has been dragging her feet in getting the statistical analysis finished. I've been trying to keep her focused, but she keeps getting distracted by other matters. I'm working with her on prioritizing. I'm not ready to fire her just yet, because she already knows the subject matter and the players. So, just to let you know I'm doing the best I can under these circumstances. With best regards, Phil.

He copied this email to Rochelle as a matter of routine. When Rochelle saw it, she immediately confronted Phil, although she caught herself and stopped short of calling him a jerk and replaced it with: "What's this all about, boss?"

> Oh, Rochelle. Calm down. Don't take it so personally. I just had to get something over to Jim. You know how it is," Phil said, laughing at her. "You're so emotional.

Rochelle was really angry now, but she just turned around and went to her desk. She took out a pad of paper, grabbed the email, and went for a short walk. She decided to send a BIFF response as an email to the project manager, with a copy to Phil.

Hi Jim, I just wanted to follow up on Phil's email from yesterday. Regarding the statistical analysis, it's almost all done. I have followed the schedule completely, even getting some parts of it done early. Now that this is the top priority of our department, I expect you will have the finished results by this Friday. Let me know if you have any questions about the statistical information. Yours, Rochelle.

Is this a BIFF?

Brief? Yes. Just a paragraph – the ideal length for most BIFFs.

Informative? Yes. She explains what *is* being done. She reassures Jim that they are on a schedule. She indicates that she is open to questions, rather than being defensive.

Friendly? Yes. She's friendly to Jim by being helpful, without being antagonistic to Phil or negative about him. Of course, Phil could consider the email to Jim itself as a hostile act, so she will need to be prepared for him to be upset.

Firm? Yes. It ends any questions about her work that were raised by Phil's email.

She also printed this out as a memo to Jim, so that it would be filed with the other important papers of the project, rather than deleted as a simple email.

> Phil was furious. "What are you doing!?!" he demanded. But Rochelle remained calm. "I just thought it was important for the project manager to know that we were working hard on this project and that he would have it real soon. I think we'll look good to him, since we are addressing his concerns about the deadline by speeding things up. Say, do you have any plans for this weekend? Anything fun you're going to do?"

Rochelle resisted the urge to make her memo a personal attack on Phil. Instead, she kept the focus on what *is being done,* not what wasn't being done or what had been done wrong. Before Phil could get too upset, she changed the subject to his weekend plans – a subject that he loved to talk about. By being calm, Rochelle was able to keep Phil from getting too heated up over her memo.

With many HCPs, changing the subject to another subject *about them* often helps keep them from getting stuck in their anger, more than directly confronting their anger – which escalates it. Of course, this doesn't always work, so you have to be careful in how you manage your HCP boss – or any HCP.

By **quickly** getting *accurate information* to the project manager, Rochelle at least created doubt in his mind, before the misinformation settled in Jim's mind as a "fact." Such facts could have quickly been passed on to other managers, so timing was very important. Putting it in writing was essential, so that when someone someday looks back in this project's file, they see Rochelle's response right next to Phil's false allegations about her. The effect of this is to at least create doubt in the reader's mind—even if the reader doesn't automatically believe Rochelle.

Without her written comment, a reader would take Phil's comments as unchallenged fact—because they sound so believable woven into his reasonable-sounding email. Of course, an employee has to be careful in going over a supervisor's head. In general, it is considered inappropriate. But if you look carefully at the way Rochelle wrote her email memo, it had several important BIFF characteristics that helped.

1. She didn't criticize Phil at all. She resisted the temptation to say that he lied or distorted the facts.
2. She didn't indicate that she was going over his head, she was merely "following up."
3. She said *what she has done* (she always was on schedule) to protect herself, rather than correcting Phil for falsely saying *what she hasn't done*.
4. She explained it to Phil as helping both of them in the eyes of the project manager.
5. She confidently changed the subject to Phil's weekend plans, which sometimes works with HCPs (but not always. You have to evaluate your own situation.)

This example demonstrates a written BIFF and a verbal BIFF. First, Rochelle wrote the BIFF to the project manager. Then, she responded to her boss' irritation with her with a verbal BIFF response. It was brief (just five sentences), informative ("just telling the project manager how we are coming along"), friendly ("we'll look good to the project manager") and firm (changing the subject to his weekend plans).

Of course, Rochelle knows how to manage her HCP boss pretty well, otherwise she might not take this approach. I don't recommend this in all cases. You have to be the judge of your own situation. (This example was taken from my book *It's All YOUR Fault!* which explains more about how Rochelle "manages" her boss, Phil.)

A Community Example

Connie is a teacher, and was talking with a small group of her students, not the entire class, and said that George Washington never really cut down a cherry tree and confessed that he did it. She said this was just a made-up example to demonstrate the idea of how honest he was. These were 4th grade students. The next day, one of the parents (of a child in her class but not in the group) confronted her behind closed doors and yelled at her and said that the teacher had traumatized her child. Connie was very upset by this incident, but the parent had bigger plans.

> "Someone" then sent an email to the local radio station with Connie's full name and place of work stating how awful she was in popping the beliefs of these little children, adding some literary license including that the teacher had said to the parent "you are lying to your child."

This email was read out on the morning show and the DJs had a good laugh at Connie's expense, which got back to her the next day. The parent then came to school and spoke to the principal and said the issue was finished for her.

Connie felt that her reputation as a teacher was tarnished and that the school was also hurt. She was understandably upset and was getting all kinds of advice from people such as: "Go to mediation with the parent." "Contact the radio station and give your side." "Ask the parent to be restrained from communicating with you."

What should she do? Let's walk through this situation in terms of a BIFF response.

Should she respond? Maybe. This is always up to the individual person. In this case, Connie feels humiliated in public and wants to respond, but doesn't want to make things worse. I recommend that she needs to respond to the same community that heard the story about her – which was partially true, partially not true and totally humiliating. It was Blamespeak about her.

To whom and how should she respond? Ideally, she should do a BIFF on the same radio show to the same audience at the same time. However, she already knows that the DJs had a good laugh at her expense. So it seems too risky to reach the community through the radio station, where they might just laugh at her again.

Instead, I recommended that she reach the community through a means she could control better. I suggested that she write a BIFF response as an open letter to parents or the school community. Ideally, it might end up in the larger community such as in a newspaper or on a website, but it would be in her own words, which she could control. If someone edited her words to change the meaning, it would be easy to expose. She wanted the whole community to know her point of view – as soon as possible. I suggested that she write a BIFF to the school community in their next newsletter. Here's what it looked like:

Dear friends of the Hill Street School community:

Last Thursday there was a radio program that said I told some students that a common historical lesson was made up and not true. While I was historically correct, I can respect that a parent would be concerned about upsetting a child's view of things at a young age, and I now regret saying it to the children without discussing it with parents first. I also want to clarify that I never said that anyone was lying to their child by not telling them the historical truth about this common story.

I want everyone to know that I share an interest in wanting children to be happy and have skills for coping with the world. I appreciate parent feedback and I am glad when parents and teachers are talking about what is best for the children. I hope that public figures will support these efforts as well.

Thank you for this opportunity to communicate with you. If anyone has any questions or concerns, please feel free to contact me.

Sincerely,

Ms. Jones

Grade 4B

She presented this proposed letter to the school principal, who was glad to see her quick response. It went out in the next school newsletter and she heard no complaints after that. The parent who was originally upset did not comment further, although Connie heard through the grapevine that this parent was not pleased with Connie's saying she never said anyone was lying to their child. But the parent now knew that Connie would respond quickly with a BIFF if any new public criticisms were made about her character. In contrast to whoever sent her name to the radio station, Connie did not publicly name the parent who had complained to her.

Is This a BIFF?

Brief? Yes. While this was more than five sentences, it was brief and appropriate, given the circumstances and the need to explain the issue to more people.

Informative? Yes. She explained three key things: 1) What had actually happened. 2) That she had never told someone (the parent – but she didn't need to be that specific) that they were lying by not telling their child the truth. 3) That she wanted parents and teachers to be able to communicate with each other for the benefit of the children and without fear of each other.

Friendly? Yes. She didn't name anyone negatively. She said she could understand a parent's concern. She said she would discuss such things with parents in the future before telling the children, if she told them things like this at all. She thanked the community for letting her communicate her view of the situation. She also invited feedback in a friendly manner.

Firm? Yes. She ended the conversation and the issue. She let people know that she had not been accurately presented to the public. She responded quickly. She told people to let her know if they had any concerns. This puts the burden on anyone who wants to complain – to complain to her personally first. It stopped any further complaints about her.

Conclusion

This chapter gave you the four key ingredients of a BIFF response to any high-conflict situation, anywhere. Keep it Brief, Informative, Friendly and Firm. It's not as easy as it sounds, but with practice and checking your BIFFs with someone you trust first, you can get better and better at it. Of course, the hardest part is avoiding the temptations of Blamespeak in your own response.

The next chapter tells you how to avoid the most common mistakes people make in their BIFFs.

CHAPTER THREE

Avoid Admonishments, Advice and Apologies

It is nearly impossible to resist the urge to write Blamespeak back, in response to a personal attack. Most people in the news can't do it, which is often why they're in the news!

Blamespeak triggers the defensive part of your brain. Before I explain the details of avoiding Blamespeak in your BIFFs, let me say a little about why our brains have such a hard time with this. It should make it easier for you to overcome the powerful urge to slip Blamespeak into your BIFFs.

Left Brain and Right Brain Conflict Resolution

Our brains are mostly divided into two hemispheres. They each have their own way of responding to conflicts, although there is some overlap. Our brains are really a combination of parts that serve different purposes. They take turns in dominating our thinking at times and generally work together – just as we have many muscles in our arms that work together rather than just one muscle.

Our brains are very flexible and the location of brain activity for different purposes varies somewhat person to person. My comments about the brain throughout this book are based on reading research, attending seminars, and seeing what works in the practice of conflict resolution. I'm not a neuroscientist, so this book is meant to be practical and general, rather than scientifically exact.

The two response methods in our brains for responding to conflict generally operate as follows:

1. **Fast defensive reacting,** which appears primarily associated with the right hemisphere of our brains (the "right brain"). This brain can respond in just a few thousandths of a second, to get us out of a bad situation before we even start to "think" about it. It's probably saved your life many times (almost falling off a cliff, escaping a bully, a run-away car, a flood, etc.), especially when you were a young child.

   It's an action-oriented response, so it doesn't have time or energy for analyzing situations. In fact, when upset enough, the *amygdala* in the right brain shuts down our logical thinking. It focuses on a fight, flight or freeze response, that sees people and situations in all-or-nothing terms, that jumps to conclusions and is driven by intense emotional energy (especially the energy of fear and anger). The amygdala acts like a smoke alarm – it gets all of your attention and doesn't leave room for slowly thinking things through.

2. **Logical problem-solving,** which appears primarily associated with the left hemisphere of our brains (the "left brain"). This brain is much more accurate in

analyzing problems – when there's time and it isn't shut off by the right brain's amygdala. This brain can look into the past objectively and compare the present situation in depth, to see how similar and how different it is.

The left hemisphere is more logical and careful. This hemisphere can take the time to plan logical responses to a situation and consider the distant future consequences, which the right hemisphere doesn't have time for in a crisis or life-threatening conflict. While intense and negative emotions are mostly processed in the right brain, the left brain tends to be the location of feelings of calmness, contentment and safety – which helps you concentrate on problem-solving.

While these two "brains" generally work together well, one is usually in charge. Which brain will dominate is generally affected by what is going on at the moment – what is happening around us. Most of the time, the left brain is dominant. But when a situation feels threatening enough or totally new, the right brain becomes dominant. Once a crisis passes or we have learned how to deal with the new situation, then we return to the left brain being dominant.

As children grow up and become adults, they become more able to tell the difference between a crisis and a minor disagreement or problem. This comes from millions of experiences, as neurons are constantly growing connections in our brains, associating problems in life to our successful strategies for solving similar problems in the past. Much of this wisdom seems to be stored in the left hemisphere of the brain.

Talking to the "Right" Brain

Blamespeak, in particular, seems to trigger our right brain response to crisis or conflict, which stops our logical thinking and makes us agitated to get ready for action. This makes sense, because Blamespeak is a personal attack, even if it's just a verbal attack. When exposed to the intensity that high-conflict people use in their Blamespeak, we get emotionally hooked (the right amygdala gets triggered) into defending ourselves. But logically there's no need to defend yourself, because "it's not about you." You don't have to prove anything. But emotionally it's hard (but possible) to override personal attacks.

We have to train ourselves to remember *during a high-conflict moment* that it's about the HCP's inability to manage his or her own emotions and behavior, so we can switch ourselves back to our logical problem-solving left brains. There's often no action we need to take at all. Of course, you may need to take action to protect yourself if there is a physical or legal threat. But you don't need to defend your own actions or prove who you are as a person.

You Can Retrain Your Brain

Brain scientists have learned that you can change your own brain by practicing learning skills. You can even learn to do the opposite of what you once did, if you practice enough. That's how it is with writing BIFF responses. Even though you may feel tempted to write a Blamespeak response, you can train yourself to weed out the Blamespeak and just write a pure BIFF. You'll be amazed at how well you can do.

You can train yourself to think, feel and say to yourself: "His comments are not really about me." "The issue's not the issue." "Her personality is the issue." And other short, quick sayings that train your brain to not react defensively.

With practice, you can keep yourself from slipping over into "fight, flight or freeze" or, if you get emotionally hooked, to bring yourself back fairly quickly. I have been teaching this skill for years and I still get emotionally hooked sometimes – but I catch myself much more quickly than I used to and usually bring myself back to being logical and calm again. Writing BIFFs can really help you with that. It helps you focus on writing carefully, rather than emotionally reacting.

You can also influence the other person's response to you. If you can respond calmly, it actually helps the other person manage their own fearful or angry response. In many ways, you can decide if the other person will react defensively or think logically about what you say – all based on your ability to send a BIFF instead of Blamespeak.

Avoid Admonishments

Admonishments are really personal criticisms by a person in a superior role, such as a parent or a judge. High-conflict people interpret them as a personal attack, for the reasons explained above.

For example, you might feel like saying to a possible HCP: "You should know better than this." "I'm surprised you would even consider such a plan." "Look in the mirror, Joe." And other comments that may sound innocent to the person giving the admonishment, but to most listeners (whether they are HCPs or not), they sound like a judgment of the whole person. If you use these expressions, you are doing what you don't want others to do to you.

The message in an admonishment is that you are superior to the person you are writing to and have the right to criticize their behavior, even if you think you are doing it gently. It's the assumption that you can judge the other person or her behavior that is the most offensive. The response will most likely be defensive, as the person tries to defend and justify their own actions. This is unnecessary and may trigger the person into their right brain defensiveness for quite a while. Just stay focused on the four parts of a BIFF response instead. It is designed to help you avoid slipping into admonishments.

Avoid Advice

This is actually the same problem as admonishments, but it often feels neutral. "I'm just trying to help with a few suggestions," you might say. Perhaps you think it's "constructive feedback." But if the person didn't ask you for feedback or suggestions, then you are treating the person disrespectfully – as though you are in a superior position to him – and he will probably attack you back if he's an HCP. High-conflict people seem to spend a lot of their day in their right brain defensiveness – don't reinforce this.

Avoid Apologies

This one is the opposite of what you would expect. While apologies are helpful with many people in many situations, they often backfire with HCPs. Instead of thanking you and that being the end of it, HCPs usually interpret an apology in an all-or-nothing manner. They think you said it was "all my fault." This reinforces their belief that it really is all your fault and they will remind you of this the next time there is a conflict (and there usually is with HCPs).

It took me a while to figure this out. One day I was counseling a couple who were in a long-term relationship. The husband seemed like a bully and the wife seemed intimidated. Suddenly, the husband pulled out a piece of paper and said, "Let me remind you of this." He went on to read:

> I'm sorry for all of the things I've said and done to disappoint you. I have disappointed myself too. I'm not as strong of a person as I thought I was, and I was wrong to criticize you and attack you for little things. I want to apologize and I hope you will accept my apology. I will try to be a better person in the future.

Then he said: "Do you remember writing this?" and he held up the well-worn paper in front of her. He had no clue that he was being a bully. He truly believed it was all her fault. After all, the paper said she agreed with him! I'm sure she wrote it in an effort to get him to calm down one day years ago. But he was too defensive to understand this and they eventually split up. He was a high-conflict person.

This is the problem with apologies to HCPs. It reinforces their all-or-nothing belief systems. I know it can be hard to resist using an apology to calm down a high-conflict person, but it often comes back to haunt you – even years later. (Of course, you can say "I'm sorry I'm late" or "I'm sorry to see you in this difficult situation." Those are social niceties, rather than taking responsibility for causing a problem.) Just be careful you aren't slipping an apology into your BIFFs.

In short, watch out for the "3 A's" described above whenever you write a BIFF. If possible, have someone else check it for you as well.

A Facebook Example

Marissa:	Got my first piercing today!
Matt:	Where is it????
Natalie:	Yeah, Marissa....how adventurous did you get?
Matt:	Can't wait to hear this one! Your dad is gonna freak!
Marissa:	Yes, my dad would freak, which is why I don't have him on Facebook! Are you ready for this?????????? It's in a place that can't be seen unless I'm in a bikini.
Aunt Debbie:	Eh hemmmmm... As your auntie speaking, I cannot BELIEVE you did this. It's not exactly MORAL!
Matt:	Well, I am proud of you Marissa! You should be able to do whatever you want with your body!
Natalie:	Well said Matt! Marissa, it's your body, your life!
Marissa:	Yes, I can do whatever I want with my body. I'm 18 now!!!!! And no one can force their morals (or lack thereof) on me!
Anya:	How dare you speak about my mom [Aunt Debbie] that way? She has more morality in her little fingernail that you'll ever have!!!!
Karrie:	Exactly! Our mom has always supported everything you do, but your snide little

comment ("lack thereof") shows exactly who you are!

Marissa: Are you for real???? Let's talk about YOUR morality, Anya and Karrie! Does your mom know everything you're doing? Hmmm???

Aunt Debbie: Marissa, how dare you?!?!?!?! Let me give YOU some advice. You need to learn from my girls. They're very good girls! And I'm not going to have your influence on them. I'm done with you! I'm unfriending you right now!!!!

But suppose that Aunt Debbie decided to use a BIFF response to Marissa *instead* of what she wrote above. Would the following be a good response? Would it be a BIFF?

Aunt Debbie: Okay, Marissa. Let's call a truce. Let's just agree to disagree. I'm done with this conversation. Bye.

Is this a BIFF?

Did she consider whether she needed to respond? She probably didn't think about it. This is an optional situation, especially since she's Marissa's aunt and will have many opportunities to communicate in the future. It's also an impossible situation to resolve when you have morality conflicts people feel strongly about. Most people in most families figure out which issues to avoid discussing in order to maintain family peace. She could have just left the conversation without saying anything, but she tried a BIFF. Did she succeed?

Brief? Yes, it's very brief, but sufficient.

Informative? Barely, but there was nothing she could really inform Marissa about. Marissa had already done her body piercing and was not asking for advice – or any information. Aunt Debbie did inform Marissa that they could "agree to disagree," which is a good adult way of ending a conflict about morality. She also informed her that she was getting out of the conversation.

Friendly? Barely, but she said, "Okay. Marissa," which acknowledged her in the conversation. "Let's just agree to disagree" is a slightly friendly way of ending a conflict. "I'm done with this conversation" is abrupt, but at least it doesn't give more negative feedback. Perhaps she could have said:

> "I don't want us to end on an angry note, Marissa, so I'm going to get out of the conversation now and look forward to hearing about your upcoming trip next time I see you. Bye for now."

Of course, this type of BIFF takes some practice and Aunt Debbie was already emotionally hooked. So I would give her credit for just getting out of the conversation without further insults.

Firm? Yes. She ended her part of the conversation by announcing she was getting out and saying "Bye." If anyone responded, she didn't want to see it and didn't see it.

Did she give admonishments, advice or apologies? (The "3 A's.") In the first discussion, before her BIFF, she tried to give Marissa advice. But when she did a BIFF instead, it didn't include any of the 3 A's. Sometimes people say "if you want any advice about such and such, let me know." However, it was clear that she wasn't being asked for advice, and people usually don't want advice in the middle of an argument – at least from the person they are arguing with. The next example addresses this issue further. But first, a comment about Facebook and other social media.

Use and Abuse of Social Media

Facebook and other social media offer the opportunity to communicate with many people at once. In many ways, this can be a good thing. However, it also offers every single one of someone's "Facebook friends" a chance to see his or her comments and respond to them immediately for all to see – including Blamespeak! And there's a lot of it in today's social media.

The original poster may have posted something completely innocuous, but the HCP responds in the form of a personal attack – usually in just a few short sentences or even just one sentence. Then it can be all out war between the two, and almost every time the "Facebook friends" get involved. People who don't even know each other join in. All of this happens very quickly and escalates rapidly.

Many people today, especially in high school, are using such social media to bully and destroy others. This gives mean girls and boys unlimited power to attack their peers – more than ever before. A BIFF response can clear up the whole thing or start to de-escalate it. The more that people use BIFF responses on the Internet, the more the HCPs will stand out as being the exception rather than the norm.

People *can* learn to catch themselves and respond with BIFFs – or not respond at all. As explained above, the amygdalas in our right brains can get emotionally hooked, but we can override the fear and anger responses by practicing reasonable responses like BIFFs. A friend using social media can step in at any time and give a BIFF, and reduce the conflict – rather than getting emotionally hooked and adding to the Blamespeak. As people learn more about HCPs, they may be less likely to want to act like one.

A Mother and Adult Son Example

The following is another example of avoiding the 3 A's. Martha, a widow, wanted to help her adult son, Jack, who was in a relationship with Andrea, who Martha described as "difficult." They had been living together for a year in another state and she felt that her son was pulling away from her because of Andrea. Martha emailed Jack about coming to visit and got the following email back:

> "Mom, you don't realize that I'm a grownup now and want to be left alone. You are interfering in my life and with my relationship with the woman I love. We are struggling financially, but we want you to know that we don't need to rely on you. Andrea has been looking for work for a long time, but in this economy it's really tough. I know you don't like her and she understands that you have lots of your own problems. You need to get a life and let us live ours."

This hurt Martha a lot. It just didn't feel like her Jack. She was certain that Andrea was turning him against her. Yet she couldn't get Jack to visit on his own. She didn't know what to do and how to respond. She finally wrote the following response to Jack's email, but asked me to review it first before sending it. She felt proud of it being brief and friendly. However, it has some issues:

> Jack, I don't want to bother you. But I think that you are being short-sighted in shutting me out of your life. I am happy that you have found "the woman you love." But your lives would be a lot easier if you would let me help out a little bit. I've got the resources to help you. I've been looking online and I think that there are jobs that Andrea could qualify for if she was willing to look outside of her usual field. Perhaps you could encourage her to consider this. She has a lot of good skills that are transferable. I really hope you will reconsider the idea of me coming for a visit. Love, Mom.

Is this a BIFF?

Brief? Yes. It's good that she resisted the urge to say she didn't have lots of her own problems. She doesn't need to defend herself and won't change Andrea's or Jack's opinions of her. But while it was only one paragraph, Martha said much more than she needed to.

Informative? Not really. She didn't focus on straight information. Instead, it was a commentary of her opinions, which will probably trigger defensiveness in

Jack – and in Andrea. If she is concerned that Andrea is having a negative influence, she's not helping make it any better.

Friendly? Yes and no. She said she was happy that he found "the woman you love." This is a double-edged sword, because these are positive words, but they sound a little sarcastic – especially putting it in quotes. She did say that Andrea had a lot of good skills. But most of it sounded intrusive, rather than friendly.

Firm? No. She is opening up several issues and conversations.

Admonishment? Yes. She admonished him for being short-sighted – a judgmental term that often triggers defensiveness, even though it was intended to help.

Advice? Yes. She's giving him advice about giving Andrea advice about finding work. She's been looking online for jobs for her son's girlfriend – not a good idea, unless she was asked to help. It definitely feels intrusive. In fact, they said they wanted to be left alone. This can easily be seen as over-bearing and will probably trigger defensiveness in both Jack and Andrea, and reinforce their resistance to having contact with Martha.

Apologies? Yes. She apologized for bothering him. This just reinforces his concern that she is intruding into his life. The next time he talks to her, he will probably say: "Mom, you ARE bothering me. Even YOU admitted it!"

A Better BIFF

There are several ways to do a better BIFF response. Here's one I suggested to Martha (since she did ask for advice).

> Dear Jack,
> Thanks for responding to my email. I respect your need for privacy and to live your own life. Since I have lost my life partner, my other family members are more important than ever. Just give me a call or send me an email from time to time. Otherwise, I get worried about you and feel like coming to see you just to make sure you're okay. If you're having a squeeze financially and want some temporary help, just let me know and I'll see what I can do. I'm glad you and Andrea are happy together. Have a nice weekend.
> Love, Mom.

Is This a BIFF?

Brief? Yes. She doesn't address the job situation at all. She doesn't defend herself about anything. Perhaps she could take out a sentence, which I'll get to below.

Informative? Yes. She's informing him that she respects his privacy; that other family members are more important now; that she feels like visiting when she doesn't hear from him; and that she can help financially – if they ask for it.

Friendly? Yes. She thanks him for responding. She says she's glad they are happy together, and avoids the hint of sarcasm in her first proposed email. She wishes them a nice weekend. This shows that she is ending on a friendly note that's not about them or about her – it's about the weekend and a common friendly closing.

Firm? Yes. It's subtle, but she is telling him that if she doesn't hear from him, the consequence is that she may feel like visiting. If he doesn't want her dropping in, then he should call her or send an email from time to time. This comment may be a bit risky, but in a way it is firm. If you don't do this, then I might do that. In other words, I'm no longer telling YOU what to do. I recognize that you have a choice. I'm telling you what I'M going to do.

Admonishment? Not directly, but see below.
Advice? No.
Apology? No.

But it could be briefer. She is still saying she can help financially. She says it in a friendly, non-advice-giving, informative way. But she doesn't need to say it at all. Jack has already told her forcefully that they don't want her help: "We don't need to rely on you." Once the other person has rejected an offer, don't keep offering it. It may be seen as an admonishment or a criticism that, "I still think you can't make it on your own."

Deciding whether to leave that financial sentence in or take it out is a judgment call for the writer. It may work, as it shows that Martha is backing off on the issue, and just making it an offer that they can accept or reject, rather than trying to interfere more directly. However, I usually think the briefer the better, so I suggested that she take it out and she did. Here's how it read now, with a couple other minor edits:

> Dear Jack,
> Thanks for responding to my email. I respect your privacy and want you to live your own life. Since I have lost my life partner, my other family members are more important than ever. Just give me a call or send me an email from time to time. Otherwise, I get worried about you and feel like coming to see you just to make sure you're okay. I'm glad you and Andrea are happy together. Have a nice weekend.
> Love, Mom.

Jack's Response

To her surprise, Martha got a phone call from Jack right after her email. He sounded like himself again. It was hard to tell if he decided on his own to call her or if Andrea told him to call so that she wouldn't try to visit. (Who knew if Andrea was listening in the background?) In either case, he appreciated her email and that she respected his new life with Andrea. Martha resisted asking too many questions and let him do most of the talking.

It was a good call and she expects that he will call more regularly. The "firm" part of her BIFF (that she feels like dropping in when she doesn't hear from him) made it clear that she was going to focus on what SHE was going to do, rather than telling him what HE had to do.

Is Andrea an HCP?

Is Andrea an HCP? Who knows? She might not be and it just might be Martha's fears or loneliness that made her think that way. On the other hand, Andrea might really be an HCP and this may become more obvious over the months or years. If she shows a lot of blaming, all-or-nothing thinking, unmanaged emotions and/or extreme behavior – like truly blocking Martha from having contact with her son – then she may be an HCP.

However, in either case, it's important that Martha use BIFF responses to maintain her relationship with her son and be supportive, without being intrusive or rejecting him altogether. From time to time, if she's concerned, she can offer assistance or information about things that help relationships in difficulty – if he seems to open that door. Some people are living with HCPs and don't realize how much information there is available for dealing with this problem. But by resisting the urge to give admonishments, advice and apologies, Martha will keep herself in a supportive role, rather than pushing him away.

Is Martha an HCP? Who knows? It's always possible that the person who's complaining about an HCP is really an HCP (and the person complained about may be, or may not be). It's too soon to tell. If she shows a lot of blaming of Andrea or Jack, with all-or-nothing thinking, unmanaged emotions and/or extreme behavior – like interfering in their lives without being asked – then she may be an HCP. As someone who reviews her BIFF responses, I can't change her. I can only give her advice when she asks for it.

It's very important not to become responsible for another person's behavior. I will give her the same information about using BIFFs, whether she's an HCP or not. I must continually remind myself: "Don't work harder than your clients!" And: "I'm not responsible for her decisions and the outcome. I'm just responsible for my part – which is giving BIFF information when I'm available and when I'm asked."

Conclusion

Responding to Blamespeak – or any difficult situation – with a BIFF can be harder than you think. That's why it's often helpful to have someone else review it before you send it out. As you can see, what you leave out is just as important – or even more important – than what you say.

The next several chapters give examples of BIFFs in many different settings. HCPs tend to focus on their intimate partners or people in authority for their *targets of blame*. The next three chapters are about using BIFFs in close relationships, then the following three chapters are about writing BIFFs if you are in a position of authority.

Of course, you might be in both situations: a close relationship with you as an authority figure. When I give seminars about managing high-conflict people in the workplace, people often tell me afterwards that this will help them with their friends and family as much as their jobs.

CHAPTER FOUR

BIFFs for Friends and Family (and Exes)

Most of us have a few high-conflict people in our extended families and friendship groups. Many also have some HCPs in their past – whether ex-spouses, former friends, or family members they avoid. These HCPs never seem to go away or they re-surface from time to time. You can use BIFFs with all of them.

This chapter includes a BIFF between a brother and a sister, who is managing the relationship; a BIFF between two friends – one of whom is reducing their friendship; and a BIFF between an ex-wife and ex-husband dealing with parenting after a divorce.

A Sister-Brother Example

Worldwide, many families have an adult HCP who is still dependent on them to solve their routine daily life problems – and this HCP angrily blames their families when they don't do what the HCP wants. I'm not talking about helping out a family member with a temporary financial or relationship problem. I'm talking about an HCP who drains their family for decades, before family members figure out how to set limits without making things worse. Using BIFF responses can be part of managing this type of family problem.

Maria's younger brother, Carlos, has been difficult his whole life. Now he has been fired from another job and lost his house. He wants Maria to deal with it and fix it for him, once again. She has been successful in her own life, but is exhausted trying to help him out. Yet she feels guilty if she doesn't.

> "Either you're with me or you're against me!" Carlos, age thirty-eight, screamed into the telephone at his sister, Maria, age forty-two. "People listen to you," he said. "It's all your fault I lost my job! You should have talked to my boss and helped clear up his false impressions of me, like I asked you to."
>
> "Carlos, you're responsible for your own life. I can't fix every problem you get yourself into. It's not my fault. It's your fault. It's your life and your responsibility," Maria replied.
>
> "See how you talk to me!" Carlos replied angrily. "It's true you never cared about me or what happened to me. You never wanted a younger brother."
>
> "That's not true, and you know it!" Maria responded in exasperation.
>
> Carlos continued. "So, since I'm losing my job, I'm also losing my house. You have to let me stay with you, again. If you'd helped me keep my job, this wouldn't be your problem. But now it is your

problem, and you have to fix it. So starting on the first of the month, I'll be moving in again."

"Don't try to blame me for this, Carlos," she replied. "And you're not moving in with me again."

After further discussion, Maria ended the call. Later, she received the following email:

MARIA, YOU JUST DON'T GET IT! YOU HAVE TO HELP ME OUT. IT'S YOUR RESPONSIBILITY AS MY SISTER, AND YOU KNOW IT. FAMILIES HELP EACH OTHER OUT IN TIMES OF NEED. AND I'M DESPERATE NOW. REALLY, REALLY DESPERATE. I DON'T SEE HOW YOU CAN FACE YOURSELF IN THE MORNING, KNOWING THAT I'M GOING TO BE LIVING ON THE STREETS WHILE YOU HAVE YOUR COMFORTABLE HOME. HOW CAN YOU SAY I DON'T MATTER TO YOU? THAT I'M JUST A SPECK IN YOUR UNIVERSE? YOU'RE SO SELF-CENTERED, MARIA, I'M ASHAMED TO HAVE YOU FOR MY SISTER. IF YOU HAD ANY SENSE IN YOUR SWELLED HEAD, YOU'D REAL-IZE THAT THERE'S ONLY ONE RIGHT THING TO DO. YOU HAVE TO LET ME LIVE WITH YOU! IT'LL JUST BE FOR A LITTLE WHILE, UNTIL I GET ON MY FEET AGAIN. DON'T BE STUPID ABOUT IT. JUST GET OVER IT AND TELL ME WHEN I CAN MOVE MY STUFF INTO YOUR GARAGE.

What should Maria do? Should she respond? It depends on how much she has already discussed this issue with him and prior limits she has set with him. If she has previously said she will not respond to his emails, then she should just ignore this. If she has not told him to stop emailing her, then she might choose to respond. After all, it's usually easier to deal with an HCP by email than in person, to give herself time to calm down before responding. In fact, it's possible that she encouraged him to email her, so she doesn't have to deal with him directly. In any case, she has chosen to respond to his emails with BIFFs from time to time.

Suppose she decides to respond. How should she respond? Should she let him move back in – again? Should she correct his extremely inaccurate statements about her? Should she point out that she never said he's just a speck in her universe?

Try writing a BIFF response to Carlos' email. Then see Maria's response.

Remember to keep it Brief, Informative, Friendly and Firm.

_____

_____

_____

_____

_____

_____

Here's Maria's response:

> Hi Carlos. I got your email. I was thinking you should get a newspaper or go online and make a list of the rental homes in your area. Do you think you would rather live with a roommate during this transition, or

get a smaller place on your own? If you want to show me the list, I can help you make some phone calls.

That's it! That's all she needed to write. It's mostly a BIFF. Notice how much she left out of that email that you may have included in yours. Here's what she left out:

- She didn't try to defend her decision to say "no." She already told him that over the phone and the "informative" part of her email clearly reinforces this by helping him look for new solutions, without rubbing his nose in the fact that she is saying "no" so that she does not put him back into his right brain defensive thinking.
- She didn't try to correct his claim that she said he was just a "speck" in her universe. She never said that. But you can't win that type of argument, so don't go there. If he can't manage his own emotions, you don't want to get him focused on *feeling like a victim* again. He carries this feeling around inside himself all the time anyway, so it's better to just avoid triggering it.
- She didn't admonish him to take responsibility – either for his job or his house. This would just trigger defensiveness.
- She didn't give him advice – or maybe she did? She "was thinking you should" look in the paper or go online. Perhaps she could have used the word "could" instead of "should": "you could get a newspaper or go online..." Nobody's perfect. If a BIFF backfires, you just make the next one better, or you don't respond – depending on the issue and your relationship.

- She certainly didn't apologize to him for anything. She stopped doing that years ago.

Here's why she included what she did:

Brief: One paragraph is generally safe to get the point across without getting into triggering issues.

Informative: While she didn't take responsibility for solving his problems, she did offer a suggestion on how to look for a place. She didn't have to do that, but in this particular case she realizes that he doesn't have the problem-solving skills that she does, so she has offered to help out in a very narrow way. After all, she really does want him to get a place to live – so he'll bother her less.

Friendly: Yes. This comes through in her helpful tone and her offer to make phone calls. It also comes through in her lack of an angry, defensive response to her brother's attacks.

Firm: Yes. The most firm part of this email is that it makes clear she is not going to allow him to live with her again. She is clearly stating that where he lives is his responsibility and the only issue is to figure out where else he is going to live. She has narrowed the discussion considerably. Next time he calls or emails her, she can just remind him of this one and ask him the same questions again about looking for a new place for himself. Or she can say: "I've already said everything I have to say on this subject."

Use of distraction: Maria has also used a method that sometimes works with upset people – distract them from their upset with a helpful or friendly comment about something else. Maria has shifted the discussion onto finding a new place for him to live and onto where he can look and how she can help him in that new task. If she reacted to his past bad behavior, or argued about why he shouldn't live with her, they would both stay stuck in a defensive argument.

This example is drawn from my book *It's All Your Fault!* For more information about how Maria dealt with Carlos, see chapter five of that book, which addresses more issues, including how she eventually set limits on future contact with Carlos.

A Friendship Example

While it's hard to reduce or end contact with a family member, it's usually easier to change a friendship. Friendships are understood to be voluntary and subject to change at any time. But HCPs form friendships that can be very intense and feel like family relationships, even if you have not known each other very long. Reducing or ending contact with an HCP friend can get as nasty as a difficult divorce in some cases.

The following is an example of how a friend, Joanie, may use a BIFF to reduce contact with an old friend, Gabriella, who has moved out of town, but still visits often. When she calls and when she visits, Gabriella spends a lot of time complaining about her parents, her health, her job, and how life always takes advantage of her. Now she has emailed Joanie about her next visit.

Hey Joanie, I'll be out next month starting on the 14th. I'll plan to stay a week and get in some beach time while you're at work. Let me tell you I am so glad to be getting away. My boss, my neighbors, my parents – you won't believe my incredibly bad luck at people who find their way into my life. Well, I guess you know. You help me deal with them so often! You are my guardian angel!

You know what my father did last week? He started yelling at me that he never wanted to see me again. Can you believe that? All I did was tell mom that she should have divorced him years ago. He just proved my point.

And my boss has been laying it on so thick. We had cutbacks and now he wants me to do the work of three people. It's starting to feel so hopeless that I've been really depressed about work. I can't stay and I can't afford to quit. And there's nothing else out there for someone my age – as you well know. Sometimes I feel like just killing myself. Just end it all! It's really hard getting up in the morning and dragging myself in to the office.

Anyway, I'll arrive on the 14th. Just wanted to give you the heads up. I'll tell you more when I get there.

xoxoxo

Your girlfriend, Gabriella

Joanie thought: How dare her friend just drop in like that? Joanie has just met a new guy, who she is really serious about. Gabriella could ruin things. So she starts to write an angry email response telling Gabriella how self-centered and manipulative she is. "Just get out of my life! You never once asked about me. And you're always threatening suicide. This gets pretty old." But she didn't finish it. She deleted it and took a break instead.

What should Joanie do? Should she respond at all? If she doesn't want her old friend visiting, then she needs to do something. But she's also afraid to say something that might put Gabriella over the edge.

Here's a possible BIFF:

> Hi Gabriella,
> Thanks for letting me know you're thinking about coming. I have to tell you that the next couple months are a really bad time for me. I have met this new guy and we are spending almost every minute together. I know you want the best for me, so I know you'll understand and not try to come and stay with me at this time. Please confirm you got this message.
> I was really sorry to hear about all the stress you have at work. I'm sure you have someone in the Employee Assistance Program (EAP) office there who could help you deal with things. Maybe they'll give you some time off for a medical leave if you're seriously depressed. I am concerned that you say you feel like killing yourself. So please let me know in the next 24 hours that you are talking to someone in the EAP office or an outside counselor or that suicide hotline number I gave you before. Otherwise, I will call your mother or the police to make sure you're okay.
> Love,
> Joanie

What do you think? Was that a good response? It certainly was a BIFF. But maybe an email response was not the best way to deal with this, especially with the talk about suicide (which is common with some HCPs). Perhaps Joanie should have picked up the phone and spoken with Gabriella directly? This depends on Gabriella's pattern of previous behavior.

Responding to Suicidal Statements

This is an important issue when dealing with HCPs. They do appear to have a higher risk of committing suicide, so you might need to get help right away. Or talk to a counselor to decide how to respond.

In this case, Joanie was familiar with this kind of talk from Gabriella and had discussed it once with a counselor. She was advised to recommend counseling services and a suicide hotline. If Joanie thought she was immediately at risk, she was told to call the police. There were many times that Gabriella had said threats like that in the email above, in the same seemingly minor way. The first time Gabriella spoke that way, Joanie had called the police.

This is always a situation to be concerned about. Get help in deciding what to do. If you ever face a situation like this and don't know what to do, get help from someone, like a suicide hotline or a counselor. Always take threats of suicide seriously.

In this case, Joanie was following a plan she had learned to use with Gabriella. But she was also burned out on Gabriella's high-conflict personality and wanted to avoid her as much as possible. She wanted to avoid calling her, because that would increase their closeness, rather than decrease it. That's why she would call Gabriella's mother or the police, rather than Gabriella, if she had concerns. Her goal is to reduce the relationship and possibly end it.

Ending a Friendship

HCPs often exhaust those around them, including strangers and friends (as well as family). Many people consider simply ending the relationship. You can do this, but it helps to do it carefully. First of all, don't be in a rush. HCPs generally have a surprisingly difficult time ending relationships, even friendships that have become almost entirely negative.

Second, understand that the high-conflict behavior of many HCPs is related to traumatic events in their childhood or growing up with a sense of entitlement. In either case, they have not learned the cause and effect of their own behavior on relationship success or failure. Thus, they do not know that relationships often ebb and flow. They tend to take an all-or-nothing approach to relationships, which means that they escalate the intensity of the relationship when they feel threatened – which is the opposite of what the reasonable friend is trying to do.

Therefore, it is often helpful to wind down the relationship more slowly without triggering their intense fears of abandonment, feeling inferior or other personality-based problem. Perhaps the best way to do this is to do what Joanie did above, namely setting firm limits on how and when Gabriella can drop in on her. She didn't talk about their relationship at all. She kept it specific to her current situation by saying No to a specific request (spending time with her).

Responding to specific situations by setting limits for that situation may help an HCP wind down their involvement to the point of ending the relationship. Therefore, I often recommend BIFFs just like the one above as the way to phase out a relationship. **Avoid writing a long letter or having a long phone call or having a long talk in person about why you want to end the relationship or friendship.** This usually intensifies the relationship, rather than wind it down. This can trigger more conflict, rather than reduce it.

If you want to tell an HCP that you are ending an intense relationship, think it through carefully. Possibly discuss it with a counselor first, so that you can plan to trigger the minimum of defensiveness. You might want to consider meeting with the HCP and a counselor to have a structured talk about ending it.

In some cases, simply reducing the relationship makes it easier to enjoy the best qualities of a friend while limiting the high-conflict qualities. In other cases, you may still want the relationship to end. However, it may be easier for the HCP to handle a reducing friendship, rather than an abrupt ending that triggers intense abandonment issues from an insecure or entitled childhood. It's generally better to let friendships with HCPs fade this way, rather than confronting the HCP with brutal honesty and ending with a dramatic (and sometimes dangerous) blow-up.

A Divorced Co-Parenting Example

It's six months since Erik and Connie's divorce was finished. But they still have routine parenting issues that come up from time to time. Some of them become fights.

Consider the following issue and then write a BIFF response for Erik to send to Connie after the email exchange below:

Erik: I'd like to have Wally on Tuesday evening, June 14th, to attend a father-son baseball game that our group has organized. I know it's usually your night, but I'd like to have this night. I'm willing to switch with another night, in order to be flexible.

Connie: Erik, you have not been helping Wally enough with his homework on his school nights! I will end your weekday overnights if you don't spend at least two hours helping him study on both of your weekday parenting nights. I want you to keep a record of the exact hours that he spends studying while he is at your house. You know I thought this parenting arrangement wouldn't work out, and it hasn't!!! And you know it!!!

             [Note that she never actually responded to Erik's request. She changed the subject. This is common with HCPs, who cannot let the other person seem to be in charge of any interaction.]

_____

_____

_____

_____

_____

_____

_____

Now, check to see if your response is Brief, Informative, Friendly and Firm.

Then, check to see if your response has any admonishments, advice and/or apologies in it.

Here's one way of writing it, but remember there is no one right way. Your BIFF needs to fit the unique current situation, which you know more about than anyone else.

Hi Connie,

Thanks for responding to my request right away. I understand your concern that Wally gets his homework done and I share that concern. I can have him work on his homework immediately after school is out, so that he has it done before the game on Tuesday. I can discuss the importance of that with him during our time together this weekend.

I understand that changing days between parents is a routine matter and I am open to changing days with you when there are special mother-son events. I believe it will make us both look good. With this new information in mind about my commitment to getting the homework done first, I will plan on picking him up from school on Tuesday, unless you tell me otherwise right away. Thanks for considering the benefits to Wally of us being flexible.

Erik

Importance of Staying Focused

One of the frequent problems with HCPs is that they often cannot answer a simple question with a simple answer. They often ignore other people's questions, and raise new issues of their own – often in an attacking manner. It's hard, but important, to stay focused and not slip into reacting.

In the example above, notice how Erik focused back onto his request and didn't get hooked by Connie's uproar about keeping track of the exact amount of time they spend on homework. He jst connected with her "concern" about homework, then brought it back to his initial subject. He was informative about how he would get the homework done, so that she could hear that he had made her concern an important issue.

Erik took a risk by planning to show up at school to pick up Wally on Tuesday, in violation of Connie's prior decision that she wouldn't switch. However, Erik presented it as new information which should lead to a new solution, rather than an angry confrontation – while still leaving the door open for her to say "no" again. He is pushing back, but respectfully and letting her know that he feels strongly about this issue.

Also, by putting all his reasons into this written BIFF response, he can show this as evidence at court some day, if necessary. Her refusal will have a price. He has made a strong case in very few words: that his request is reasonable, that he would do the same for her and that such exchanges are routine.

If she rejects his plan, then he can inform her that he will not challenge that, by saying: "Ok. See you Saturday for our next exchange."

If someone keeps responding and tries to keep the conflict going, just say: "I've said all I'm going to say on this subject. Have a good weekend." Or something like that. Then stop responding all together if you keep getting more texts or emails.

Conclusion

The BIFF examples in this chapter can be used for any family or friend situation. The first and last examples showed ways of managing a generally unavoidable relationship, such as one with a sibling or the co-parent of your child. The second example showed ways of reducing a friend relationship, which also could lead to ending the relationship if necessary.

All of these are examples, not absolute rules, of how you can respond to a variety of difficult situations with an HCP using BIFF responses. It is a balanced approach, which is not mean or confrontational, yet helps set limits and focus on solving problems rather than just reacting to reactions to reactions.

Two important new principles were presented in this chapter that are related to BIFFs. First, suicidal statements are common with some HCPs and must always be taken seriously. However, this does not mean that you allow yourself to be manipulated on issues. Police or other qualified people need to be contacted to take protective action. Sometimes you can use a BIFF as part of dealing with this, but often you need to immediately call for help. People who commit suicide usually tell someone they feel like it beforehand. Don't ignore this possibility.

The second new principle is the importance of staying focused when you are dealing with an HCP. They have great difficulty letting others take the initiative in conversations and don't like it when you set limits with them. They often totally ignore the requests of others and raise extreme demands of their own – often in the form of a counter-attack, such as Connie did with Erik. Expect this behavior and try not to react and get distracted. Just respond with a BIFF in writing or in person. This will help you "contain" the situation, rather than make it worse.

CHAPTER FIVE

Neighbors

Neighbor personalities come in all shapes and sizes. Some HCP neighbors are friendly at first, then get nasty. Others are difficult from the start. More and more, neighbors are addressing problems by email. But BIFFs may be useful in conversations as well. In this chapter we address a BIFF to a neighbor and a BIFF response by a community manager of a homeowners' association.

A Neighbor Example

Kimberly and her husband, Victor, lived slightly downhill from their neighbor Jake in Lakeview. Kim and Vic had lived there for about ten years when Jake moved in. Over the months, they would give a friendly wave to Jake and they had exchanged phone numbers and email addresses at a neighborhood picnic by the lake. After about six months, Kim and Victor received an email from Jake demanding that they cut off the tops of their trees, so that his view of the lake was completely unobstructed. Kim and Vic walked up to see the view from beside Jake's house and observed that their trees barely affected the view – in fact, in a few years they might make a nice frame on both sides of Jake's view of the lake. So they kindly emailed back that there was no need to cut their trees. From their observations, there was no problem.

Then, they received the following email from Jake:

Hi Kim and Vic,

You don't know what you are talking about! Your trees are blocking the view that I paid good money for. I'm not going to just sit idly by while you interfere with my property rights. Your trees are a nuisance and the tops must be cut off, or I will bring legal action against you. I have already consulted with an attorney who says I could force you to remove your trees if you do not agree with me.

When I first moved into Lakeview, I thought you were nice, considerate people. Now I know that you are two of the most insensitive people I have ever met. You have no respect for the feelings or rights of others. On top of that, you are willing to lower my property values with no effect on your own. I have spoken to two other neighbors who agree with me that you should cut down the tops of your trees. This is a very simple request and you are being very inconsiderate to ignore me this way.

Your frustrated neighbor,

Jake

Kim and Vic's Response

How should Kim and Vic respond? Do they need to respond? After all, they had already said "No" to Jake's request.

I believe that they should respond, as Jake is escalating the issue rather than accepting their response, and Jake is an important person in their lives – their neighbor who lives just up the hill. Would the following be a good BIFF?

> Hi Jake,
> We are also frustrated. After living here for ten years we have never had such a problem with a neighbor. We don't know who you're talking to or whether you just made them up, but we know the neighbors and no one has mentioned such a concern about trees to us before. We strongly advise you not to try to turn any neighbors against us. It will backfire on you. We looked at the view by your house, and our trees are not a problem. So we ask you to just leave us alone and find something better to do with your time. Otherwise, we will be talking to our attorney about taking action against you. We are respected in Lakeview and we refuse to be treated in this manner.
> Thank you,
> Kim and Vic

Is this a BIFF Response?

Brief? Kim and Vic's response was just one paragraph, which is a good length for most BIFFs.

Informative? It did inform Jake that they did not agree, but it did not focus on neutral, factual information. It sounds like a defensive response, with their opinions about Jake perhaps making up fictitious neighbors and threatening legal action themselves. Such a defensive response will trigger an even greater defensive response from Jake.

Friendly? They did say "Thank You," but after criticizing Jake and threatening him. The overall tone is clearly an angry one and not a friendly message that will have a calming effect.

Firm? In a sense, they tried to end the conversation by asking to be left alone. But saying it this way will invite a strong response from Jake.

Admonishments? Yes, they told him to "find something better to do.

Advice? Yes, they advised him not to attempt to turn the neighbors against them.

Apologies? No.

Let's see if this could be done as a BIFF. You can try writing one before looking at the next page. Remember, there are many ways to write a BIFF.

_____

_____

_____

_____

_____

_____

_____

_____

_____

_____

Kim and Vic's Re-Write

Hi Jake,

We were saddened to see that this has become a frustrating issue. We want to have happy neighbors and we want to be happy neighbors too. We don't want this to grow as a problem between us, so we have a suggestion. There is a community mediation service in Lakeview and we suggest that the three of us have a meeting with one of their mediators. They have been successful at resolving many neighbor disputes in Lakeview. Here is their phone number: 555-9876. If you would like to call them and find out about their services, we would be open to meeting together. If you would like us to call them first, we would also be willing to do that. Just let us know.

Regards,

Kim and Vic

Is this a BIFF Response?

Brief? Yes, one paragraph.

Informative? Yes, it presented information about a solution to their problem, without criticizing, demanding or threatening anything.

Friendly? Yes, they let Jake know they did not want him to be frustrated, but happy instead. They gave him a choice about calling the mediation service or having them do it.

Firm? Somewhat. They didn't close the conversation, because theirs was a decision that could be made jointly – whether to use the mediation service. But they narrowed their email to focus on two choices regarding a solution – Jake could call or they could call. This was a friendly way of addressing the problem, so that they did not seem be demanding that he call and they did not seem to be rushing to influence the mediator first. Giving the other person a choice of two options for problem-solving is often a good way of being friendly.

Admonishments? No, they didn't say anything about Jake or how he should spend his time.

Advice? No, they made a suggestion for a shared solution, rather than telling him what to do.

Apologies? No. They said they were saddened to read about his frustration, but they did not say that they were sorry for anything that they had done.

Should they keep communicating by email? This is an important question in any close relationship, which can include close neighbors. We all know how emails can quickly escalate into disrespectful Blamespeak and it may become dangerous for neighbors to let this happen. And with the advent of Facebook, Twitter and other social media, these situations can escalate almost instantaneously and involve a lot more people. In most cases, it's better to speak directly. However, if you are dealing with a high-conflict dispute or a potentially high-conflict neighbor, it may be best to talk with an experienced person, such as a mediator, rather than risk a dangerous confrontation growing out of the dispute. With that in mind, the above response looks like a good BIFF.

Negative Advocates

But suppose that Jake really did talk to the neighbors and told them how unreasonable Kim and Vic were. Suppose that he sent two of their neighbors an email. This is a common behavior of HCPs, who often aggressively recruit "negative advocates" (other people to advocate for their negative solutions, emotions and behavior) in an escalation of their conflicts. Otherwise, they fear they may "lose" the dispute without an army of advocates on their "side." They automatically assume that everyone else is doing this, so they are often fast and aggressive in the process of recruiting negative advocates.

Of course, they don't see that they are doing this and will deny it if confronted about it. It seems natural and ordinary to them to find advocates, rather than to find positive solutions between the parties involved. And it's especially easy to do these days with Facebook, Twitter and other social media. You can add and lose friends instantly with the simple click of a mouse! This gives HCPs a great feeling of power and they often use it instead of solving problems.

Jake didn't hesitate for a minute after receiving Kim and Vic's email, before he sent an email to the two neighbors with a copy of Kim and Vic's BIFF response. He also copied Kim and Vic on his email, as if to show them how bad they would look to the neighbors if they didn't do what he wanted.

Hi Joel and Max,

The other day I spoke to you about the tree problem and you were both sympathetic to my problem about my blocked view. After courteously asking Kim and Vic to remove the tops of their trees, look at the response that I get. They take no responsibility for this problem and want to involve strangers in our neighbor issue. I can't believe it! I hope you will help me convince Kim and Vic that they need to just get this done. It's going to ruin all of our property values if we let them do this to any of us without any respect for their neighbors.

Respectfully,

Jake

Responding to Potential Negative Advocates: The Neighbors

Remember Jane's response in Chapter Two when her ex-husband wrote something to her friends and family? The same kind of response can work here.

But first, should Kim and Vic respond? My experience is that it is very helpful to respond to potential negative advocates as quickly as possible. If you don't, then they may absorb the emotions of the HCP and come to believe that he is being reasonable and you are not.

I recommend responding in the same format as they received the negative comments about you. In other words, responding by email to an email; by letter to a letter; by Facebook to a Facebook posting; tweet to tweet; and by public comment to a public comment. This helps prevent the emotions of the moment from taking hold. Your quick BIFF response can cancel out the negativity and encourage potential negative advocates to avoid getting caught up in a conflict they do not fully understand. Sometimes, negative advocates become positive advocates and assist in resolving the conflict. In other cases, they avoid the conflict.

Keep in mind: Negative advocates are usually emotionally hooked but uninformed. The way to deal with them is usually to inform them, as soon as possible. However, in some cases you will not have any access to potential negative advocates or it will be best to just leave them alone. You will need to weigh each situation yourself.

Of course, you should always consider consulting with someone else about whether or how to deal with potential negative advocates in any situation. Seeking consultation is totally different from seeking negative advocates, as you are getting assistance to help you manage a problem, rather than seeking advocates to take sides and blame another person.

With this in mind, try writing one of your own BIFF responses to the neighbors, then look at the example.

_____

_____

_____

_____

_____

_____

_____

_____

_____

Hi Joel and Max,

We see that Jake has contacted you about a disagreement we have about our trees. As you can see from our email he forwarded to you, we have made a suggestion for resolving this issue. If you have any questions or concerns, we hope that you will feel free to talk to us at any time. As you know, we have always enjoyed our peaceful neighborhood and look forward to quickly solving any problems as they arise.

Regards,

Kim and Vic

Is it a BIFF?

Brief? Yes.

Informative? Yes, about how the dispute is being addressed, and that Kim and Vic are not seeking to involve them.

Friendly? Yes, in that it invites them to raise any questions or concerns directly with Kim and Vic.

Firm? Yes, in that it intends to end the discussion.

After receiving a BIFF like this, most neighbors (and family, friends and co-workers) will do everything they can to avoid getting further involved. If Kim and Vic had not sent their BIFF quickly in the same format, there is the risk that Joel and/or Max could get drawn into absorbing Jake's emotions and viewpoint on this issue. After several conversations, it would become much harder – but not impossible – for Kim and Vic to undo all of this negativity about them. I'm sure you've seen this happen from time to time – perhaps to yourself or others you know. A quick BIFF response can make a big difference, as it is Informative – the secret weapon against negative advocates (who are emotionally hooked but uninformed).

Homeowners' Associations and HCPs

More and more people live in communities with a governing association, whether a condo organization or a homeowners' association. HCPs often show up, either as community members with numerous complaints at meetings and/or sometimes members of the homeowners' association board. Rumors can spread quickly among neighbors, and a well-run association will stay on top of problems before they escalate. BIFFs can help in this process.

A Homeowners' Association Example

Many homeowners' associations have a Community Manager who is responsible for supervising much of the day-to-day staff and issues in the community. Scott is one such manager and he gets many complaints and is generally skilled at managing them. However, one community member in particular appears to be an HCP. She often comes to association meetings with complaints to the Board. She often likes to complain about Scott to the Board. At one meeting she had the following to say:

> Scott is not doing his job. Almost every day I have to pick up litter near the office and he has allowed his special friends to have exceptions to the CC&Rs regarding their fences. Such favoritism should not be tolerated, but the Board does not seem to care about this. You do not even seem to be paying attention to these important matters. I am considering bringing a formal complaint. You need to look into this immediately. The next two community members agree with me. We will give you a week.

How should the Board President (who is running the meeting) respond? Should she defend the Community Manager? Should she immediately open an investigation? Should there be a response at all? Should there be a response at the end of the meeting, after all community members have had a chance to speak on all subjects?

When to Respond to a Community?

As described at the end of the last example, a quick response is best. Otherwise, everyone at this community meeting will start to wonder if it's true that Scott is not doing his job. Do you think the following might be a good BIFF response?

> Board President: Thank you for bringing that to our attention. I was not aware of any concern about litter by the office or favoritism regarding exceptions to the CC&Rs regarding fences. I will look into that right away and post a community notice on our website with the results. We value community feedback and like to solve problems right away. Now we will hear from the next community member.

Is it a BIFF?

Brief? Yes, so brief that he made these comments almost in passing, as the next speaker was called upon.

Informative? Yes, as he informed the member that no such problems had been raised before. This comment was for the community's benefit as well as the member, as he implied that this was likely to be a very minor or non-existent problem, without directly insulting the member. He also said it would be looked into immediately and where the results could be found. He chose not to say the results would be presented at a future community meeting, to avoid giving more attention to this potentially non-existent problem and to avoid publicly embarrassing the member if that was the outcome. Of course, if there was a problem, it could still be raised by the Board at the next meeting. The BIFF response above keeps all of these options open.

Friendly? Yes, as he thanked the member and said the problem would be addressed. He added that community feedback is valued, so that the member and the other community members present would not feel at risk of being treated with disrespect if they raised minor or questionable issues. Such friendliness builds stronger communities.

Firm? Yes, he closed the discussion saying it would be looked into, then called the next speaker.

All of this was communicated in a quick, respectful BIFF response. Simple, but not easy.

Conclusion

As in the previous chapter, these BIFF examples can be used in any situation. In addition, the neighbor example included a look at the common problem of negative advocates, who get hooked into the dispute by HCPs. Both examples demonstrated how informing potential negative advocates can help reduce the chance that they will remain negative and may even leave the dispute or help in solving problems. The Homeowners' Association example also showed how a BIFF response can be done verbally, instead of in writing, and by a representative of any organization that is being blasted by an HCP for little or no reason. **Remember, with HCPs the issue's not the issue – the personality is the issue.**

CHAPTER SIX

In the Workplace

Today's workplace can be anywhere, which means that more and more work is done (or not) online. This also means that hostile emails are everywhere. Some people can restrain themselves at work, but many others can't.

This chapter includes an employee dealing with a high-conflict supervisor, a manager dealing with a high-conflict employee, and a Human Resources professional dealing with a former employee.

A High-Conflict Supervisor

Lea worked at the company for two years before her supervisor left and another one, Cynthia, took over. There were immediate problems for the whole staff with Cynthia, but she particularly bullied Lea. One day Lea was out sick with some type of stomach flu and her daughter also stayed home with the same problem. When she returned, she received the following email from Cynthia:

Well, *Princess* Lea, I hope you're proud of yourself for taking off on the day the rest of us had the most work to do all year. We had to get that presentation prepared and you knew it! I will expect to see a note from the doctor first thing tomorrow morning to confirm that you were sick! You think you're so special sometimes and this is not the time or the place to stop pulling your weight in the office. If this happens again, there will be certain consequences. Perhaps someone else would be better in your position.

Cynthia Jones, Unit Manager

Lea was really upset and didn't know how to respond. So she prepared the following email reply, but decided to wait and think about it a little more before sending it.

Dear Cynthia,

I am shocked at your accusations against me. For your information, I have only missed two days of work in the past year, while I already know that you have taken more sick days than that yourself. You have a double standard for us in this unit and it is making it hard for all of us to work with you. You waste time chit-chatting, while you expect us to be on task every second. You take questionable time off, while you demand that I prove I was really sick. Well I was, but it passed in a day, so I didn't go to the doctor. If it's the policy of this unit to require a doctor's note for a single day missed, then you need to post that policy. I know that your favorite employee was out for a day a couple weeks ago and you didn't require such a note from him. If you don't stop this harassment of me, I will make a formal complaint against you to our division manager. Leave me alone!

Is This a BIFF?

No. It's too long and filled with statements that will trigger defensiveness in Cynthia and a further escalation of the issue, unnecessarily. Lea may be totally justified in each of her statements, but it will not solve any problems and her work environment will worsen – especially if Cynthia really is a high-conflict person as Lea describes.

But there may be the seeds of a BIFF response in what Lea has written. Try to write a BIFF, using information in Lea's first attempt. Give it a try, then see how it compares to the one below.

_____

_____

_____

_____

_____

_____

_____

_____

_____

_____

_____

_____

A BIFF Response to the Supervisor

Here's one way to do a BIFF response to Cynthia's bullying email:

> Dear Cynthia,
> Thanks for letting me know your concerns about my absence yesterday. I was sick with stomach flu from something I ate. My daughter had the same illness and was pretty miserable herself. Fortunately, I was able to keep it to one day of missed work and pushed myself to get back to work today, even though I wasn't feeling 100% better, because I knew how important this presentation is to our unit. I don't have a doctor's note and I was unaware that one was required for a single day's absence. I only missed one other day of work in the past year and was not informed that I needed a note last time. If this is a requirement, please let all of us know. I look forward to assisting with this presentation, as I know it will make our unit shine.
> Regards,
> Lea

Is this a BIFF?

Brief? Yes, fairly brief. It could be a little shorter, but in this case it gives Lea a chance to sound friendly by adding some personal touches, such as her daughter was "pretty miserable" and the upcoming presentation will "make our unit shine." If she was too short and curt in her response, it might sound unfriendly or hostile,

which you want to avoid when you have to work close-
ly with someone in the future – especially your boss!

Informative? Yes. Lea gets to explain that she only
missed two days this year; that she pushed herself to
come in despite feeling not completely well; that she
wasn't asked for a doctor's note the previous time; and
that she wanted to help the unit shine. All of these
were presented as straight information, rather than as
accusations of bad behavior by Cynthia.

Friendly? Yes. As described under Brief, she added
some friendly comments to make it seem like a relaxed
and routine conversation. While her last sentence
was not necessary in terms of information, it will help
shift the focus to the positive and distract from the
negativity about the past.

Firm? Yes. Lea basically put an end to the conversation
with a request for a policy notice and a friendly note
about helping the unit to shine.

Responding to Narcissistic Characteristics

Does Cynthia have a narcissistic personality pattern? If she
might, two things can be important to include in BIFF
responses like this:

1. **It helps to focus on policies**, even as an employee.
   This is a subtle way of setting limits on a narcissistic
   boss who makes up her own rules, without directly

challenging her. Direct challenges should be avoided like the plague with narcissists – they can't handle it and will attack you for it and make your life miserable for a long time.

2. **They really need buttering up**, so emphasize something that will make the supervisor look good. In this case, Lea emphasized that the presentation will make Cynthia's unit shine. That shifts Cynthia's attention to think about something rewarding for her.

This type of approach has worked well in dealing with many narcissistic bosses – perhaps the most common workplace complaint we get at High Conflict Institute. It's a friendly carrot and stick approach: "I will focus on policies which we all including the supervisor need to follow and I will help make your department look good." This tells Cynthia not to bully Lea, and that Lea can help Cynthia's reputation in the eyes of others in the company.

Resist Pointing Out Projection

High-conflict people often "project" their own behavior onto others. This means they don't even recognize that they are doing this. In Cynthia's case, she appears to be projecting her own self-centered "princess" characteristics onto Lea, where they don't fit. Lea doesn't act that way or see herself that way, and others have never given her that type of feedback. That's because it's not about her – it's really about Princess Cynthia. But Lea can't directly point this out and there's nothing Lea needs to defend. So she ignored it altogether. This is one of the hardest things to do when you're dealing with a narcissistic boss, but it will make your BIFFs simpler and more likely to end the conversation.

A High-Conflict Employee

Marty comes to work late, parks in other people's reserved spots and is often slow at getting his projects done. Yet he has some brilliant high-tech skills that the company needs. When his manager, Harry, has tried to carefully address this with him, he goes ballistic and says, "Marty rocks and you know it!" Then he walks away.

Harry is preparing a short letter which he will hand to Marty the next time they meet, so it doesn't matter if he walks away again. How does this look to you?

> Dear Marty,
> You are a valued employee with XYZ Technologies. I want you to succeed here and you have made several valuable contributions. The following are a few pointers that you need to pay attention to right away:
>
> 1. Management is putting pressure on me to enforce our work hours more thoroughly, so that there will be no exceptions starting now. Please make sure to get here on time every day.
> 2. The Reserved parking spots are limited to top management, who often have to come and go all day long. If this is a problem, please talk to John Smith about whether these rules have any flexibility.

3. The timing of our projects is becoming more important, so that each of us must abide by our personal completion dates for each one. Production and Promotion departments have strict schedules and the pressure is building on us as our competition is growing.

If you have any questions about any of these three expectations, let me know immediately. I think we can accomplish our goals and continue to be the leader in this field if we stick together. I appreciate the cooperation of everyone on our team and I told upper management that we would work hard together regarding these issues.

Sincerely,

Harry

Unit Manager

Is it a BIFF?

Brief? Yes, for this purpose. It makes three simple points that need attention.

Informative? Yes. It explains the rules and the reasons for them in non-accusatory terms.

Friendly? Yes. There is no criticism stated – although a little might be implied. Overall, Harry has done a good job of focusing on future expected behavior, without emphasizing or criticizing the past.

Firm? Yes. He has stated that everyone must follow these guidelines and expectations. He explained that he is under pressure, so that is why the unit is under pressure and everyone's cooperation is needed.

Indirect Confrontations

Now you might argue that Marty has acted badly and therefore should have all of his bad behaviors pointed out to him. You could try such a direct confrontation and if it works, that's great. However, it almost always fails with high-conflict people, because their defensiveness takes over and they don't learn from it. Instead, a different approach is needed which is less likely to trigger their defensiveness and more likely to get the desired future behavior.

I call this approach an "indirect confrontation." It has two basic parts:

1. **Desired future behavior:** You inform the person of the future behavior you would like to see, without criticizing the person. You avoid bringing up the past, unless you are required to do so at this point – in which case you emphasize the future after sufficiently addressing the past. Ideally, these indirect confrontations are done early enough at a low level, that you do not need to take disciplinary action. In Marty's case, if he didn't improve, then formal progressive discipline would begin.

2. **Based on a policy reason:** Rather than saying that Marty is a jerk, insensitive, or irresponsible, Harry

simply stated the policy reasons for the desired future behavior. This avoids a lot of defensiveness. If there wasn't a policy, one could be created. High-conflict people are good at finding policy loopholes in organizations, so they may actually benefit the organization in this regard. This keeps the focus on logical reasoning, rather than on personal defensiveness.

If your goal is to see an improvement in behavior from a high-conflict person, then indirect confrontations will often help you a lot. The average person doesn't need such careful words, as they can balance negative feedback with logical reasoning – and grow from it. This is just a major issue for high-conflict employees.

A Terminated Employee

Roberta was terminated after a long progressive discipline process, with repeated failure to comply with the company rules. There had been several incidents in which she was believed to have harassed other employees, although none of the incidents ever resulted in legal claims (fortunately). After being counseled by the Human Resources department several times without any change in her behavior, she was terminated. Since she was not a member of a union and there was no contract for her position, she was let go "at will" of the company, without justification necessary (although the company had plenty of it).

Jerry is the Human Resource manager who dealt with her in the termination process. Jerry has remained in contact with Roberta by email, in order to be helpful to her and to help keep her calm during this transition in her life. Here is an example of the emails he gets from her:

> Hi Jerry,
>
> I had another job interview this week. This is good, because my medical benefits are running out, thanks to you. You had no right to ruin my career and make it impossible for me to get a good letter of reference. Your corrupt company will be exposed sooner or later. By the way, I need a copy of that last list of job duties that I had. I've asked you three times for it, and you refuse to respond. Let me know if I need to drop by to pick it up.
>
> Your old friend,
>
> Roberta

Here's the email that Jerry is thinking of sending. What do you think? Is it a BIFF?

> Hi Roberta,
>
> First of all, it will not benefit you at all to make threats about "exposing" our company. We have done nothing wrong and are ready to refute any claims you may raise against us.
>
> I was not aware of you ever asking for a list of your job duties. Please see it attached.
>
> As a reminder, you are not allowed to return to our company, nor allowed to set foot on our grounds. We will have you arrested if you attempt to do so.
>
> I hope that this message is clear.
>
> Sincerely,
>
> Jerry Butler
>
> Human Resource Manager

Is it a BIFF?

Brief? Yes, it's fairly brief.

Informative? Yes and No. It goes beyond straight information (see "3 A's?" below) and sounds defensive.

Friendly? Not really. It focuses on her negativity, unnecessarily. Nowhere does he make an attempt to connect in a friendly way. You can tell that he's pretty angry with her, by emphasizing the negative and purely setting limits, rather than trying to have a calming influence on her. While his anger is understandable, it won't help him bring an end to having conversations with her.

Firm? Yes, somewhat. It sounds very firm, in that he is telling her the consequences of various actions. However, it's not firm in terms of ending the conversation. It is defensive and will reinforce her defensiveness with him and trigger even more communication from her.

3 A's Admonishment, Advice, Apologies? Yes. Jerry advises or admonishes her to not make threats. "It will not benefit you." This adds nothing useful, makes it longer and risks triggering more defensiveness. While he makes it very clear that there is nothing to apologize for, he is just feeding the conflict and doesn't need to say this at all.

While the above first attempt was not a BIFF, there may be the seeds of a BIFF response in what Jerry has written. Try to write a BIFF, using information in Jerry's first attempt. Give it a try, then see how it compares to the one below.

_____

_____

_____

_____

_____

_____

_____

BIFF Response to Terminated Employee

Dear Roberta,

I'm glad you're making progress and getting interviews. I really want you to find a company that's a good fit for you.

I am attaching a copy of your job duties. I hope that helps!

Best wishes!

Jerry

Is it a BIFF?

Brief? Yes, it's very brief.

Informative? Yes, it explains he wants her to find a good fit, and he attaches her job duties. There is nothing in this that sounds defensive or would trigger defensive-ness for her.

Friendly? Yes, he expresses his positive wishes and responds to her request with straight information.

Firm? Yes, in that he does not invite a response to anything. He has put an end to that conversation, even though he knows there will be more.

3 A's (Admonishment, Advice, Apologies)? No. Jerry doesn't give any advice or admonishments. Instead, he gives encouragement and hope. He also has nothing to apologize for.

Why Stay in Touch?

The BIFF approach focuses on "containing" communication, rather than eliminating it. When a high-conflict employee has been terminated, there is very likely to be left-over, unresolved feelings that the HCP may not be able to handle on his or her own. Sending hostile emails to the former company is one way HCPs stay in touch.

This is far better than having a disgruntled employee showing up at the workplace or spreading rumors in public. These emails provide a forum for the HCP's frustrations, and the H.R. manager can "contain" the communication, without trying to eliminate it. He ignores all of the emotion-al hooks she has put out for him. This approach takes almost no time on the H.R. manager's part, yet it helps the compa-ny avoid lawsuits, publicity and chaos.

Should You Ignore Threats?

No. You need to protect yourself. But you generally want to avoid mentioning them in your BIFF, for the reasons explained below.

Protecting yourself: Of course this subject requires specific knowledge of the employee or former employee. In this case, Roberta threatens to expose the company and threatens to come back to the workplace. In the BIFF response I have suggested above, Jerry completely ignores both of these threats. *However*, he tells company security that she has said she might "drop by" and he has made efforts to eliminate the reason for her to do so – namely providing the list of job duties without her needing to come and get it.

Avoid mentioning threats in your BIFF: In general, HCPs have a hard time managing their thoughts and feelings. They will think more about the subjects that you remind them about. Ironically, it's like saying "Don't think of a pink elephant." Of course, you automatically think of one – it's unavoidable.

So just imagine telling an HCP: "Don't you even think of coming back on company property – there will be consequences." The person will immediately envision coming back on company property, which may stir up emotions and ideas related to coming back. The drama of the consequences may actually be appealing, rather than discouraging to them. For example, she may get excited about being arrested and led away with TV cameras rolling – even though this is very unlikely.

In a sense, you decide what the HCP will think about next by how you respond. A well-contained BIFF response may help the HCP contain herself.

Conclusion

In today's world, the workplace is where many HCPs deal with their relationship issues. While the average worker or manager is focusing on work problems, the HCPs are focusing on their own internal difficulties and trying to resolve them with those who have to be close to them every day. Whether a supervisor, an employee or a former employee is an HCP, the same general principles apply in how you respond to them in writing and verbally. It may help to teach this method throughout the workplace, so that everyone realizes its benefits and can resist the urge to escalate HCPs. This may make it easier on everyone (including the HCPs).

CHAPTER SEVEN

Business and Professions

Businesses today have many opportunities to deal with HCPs as customers, suppliers, contractors, partners and in negotiations over future business relationships. Professionals face similar situations, as they often operate as small businesses and deal with HCPs on a regular basis.

All businesses and professions create expectations, but the expectations of HCPs are often very unrealistic. This can lead to angry outbursts, customer relations complaints, consumer affairs complaints, licensing board complaints, rumors among colleagues, bad publicity and lawsuits. BIFFs can help you manage risks and reduce the distraction of endless emotional issues with HCPs.

The goal isn't to avoid all HCPs in business and professional work – you can't ever succeed at that because most HCPs are not obvious at the beginning. Instead, the goal is to contain the emotional challenges and stay focused on the services that you want to provide. When handled correctly, most HCPs can be satisfied customers, productive employees and even sources of future work.

This chapter will include BIFFs for a delivery problem, a high-conflict business client, a high-conflict business partner and a public relations BIFF.

A Business Delivery Example

The following was by text message:

Todd: Still waiting for that delivery.

Sandy: Todd...if you hadn't screwed it up in the first place, you'd have had it by now.

Todd: YOU were the one who screwed up – not ME.

Todd: And YOU can explain it when Rick sees the cost overruns. YOU CAN EXPLAIN THAT YOU WERE THE F'ING MORON WHO'S RISKING FUTURE CONTRACTS WITH HIS COMPANY!

Sandy: I clearly did NOT screw up and I have proof that it was you. Can't you see for one single second that it was your fault???

This is such a common Blamespeak conversation that it's hard to tell if either Todd or Sandy is an HCP or just stressed out. In any case, both of them could have used a BIFF at any time. Suppose that Todd had started out trying a BIFF. Would this have worked?

Todd: Hey Sandy, I'm still waiting for that delivery. Do you have an estimated time of arrival? Thanks!

Is it a BIFF?

Brief? Yes.

Informative? Yes. He is informing Sandy that it still has not arrived. He simply asks for information about when it will.

Friendly? Yes. He gives a greeting and says "Thanks."

Firm? Yes. He makes a narrow request for information, without opening up a discussion.

Sandy could have done the same thing, by using a BIFF for his first response to Todd's statement:

Sandy: Okay, I'll look into it. I thought it would be there by now.

But suppose that he had already told Todd that Todd "screwed up." How could Sandy have responded to Todd's meltdown? Would this be a BIFF?

Sandy: Okay, Todd. I know the delay's upsetting. For your information, I sent it Express two days ago, so you should have it today – tomorrow at the latest.

Is it a BIFF?

Brief? Yes. It could be briefer, but too brief can feel abrupt. This is a good length.

Informative? Yes. He is informing Todd about when he sent it and when it should arrive.

Friendly? Yes. He says "Okay, Todd" and lets Todd know he understands he's upset. Then he gives him helpful information.

Firm? Yes. He ends the discussion.

3 A's (Admonishment, Advice, Apologies)? No. He avoids apologizing, although Todd says it's Sandy's fault. Even if Sandy did something wrong, he should focus on the solution and avoid feeding a likely HCP with ammunition by apologizing.

A High-Conflict Client Example

For many years, divorce mediation has been a growing alternative to going to court to get divorced. One experienced divorce mediator received the following letter from a dissatisfied client:

Dear Sir:
You met with us on Sept. 9th for our divorce mediation and we scheduled another meeting for Sept. 23rd.

We are now cancelling that meeting, because both my wife and I (and my attorney) believe that you did not handle our mediation properly. We accomplished nothing in our first meeting. I paid for the mediation and I would like my money back. Please respond promptly. We have found another mediator who does it correctly.

Sincerely,

Disgruntled Client

The mediator was surprised. He'd never received such a letter before. He recalled that this was a client who came late, took phone calls on his cell phone and made several comments toward his wife. The mediator was tempted to say this in a reply. However, he sent the following BIFF response in a letter (after having it reviewed), since the client had communicated by letter:

Dear Client,

Thank you for your letter expressing your concerns about our mediation session. After doing nearly 1000 divorce mediation cases and teaching a course in mediation at two law schools, I have learned that people have different styles of providing mediation services. I am glad that you have found a mediator that fits for you. Best wishes in completing your divorce.

Sincerely,

Mr. Mediator

Is it a BIFF?

Brief? Yes. It's one paragraph, which is enough for most BIFFs.

Informative? Yes. He informs the client that he has a lot of experience doing his job, is respected in the community and that different styles could be the problem, rather than poor service.

Friendly? Yes. He thanks the client for his letter and ends with "Best wishes."

Firm? Yes. He makes it clear that he did nothing wrong and that their communication is finished.

Interestingly, the mediator never heard from him again. You may wonder why he didn't tell the client directly that he would not refund his money. He believed that he had performed his services satisfactorily and that his letter made it clear that he didn't owe a refund (or an apology).

Also, the mediator didn't want to make him *think* about a refund any further, as raising the issue and then rejecting it was more likely to reinforce the client's negative mood. This BIFF letter was the least likely approach to trigger his defensiveness, and it appears to have helped him let go. If the client followed up with a more demanding letter, then the mediator could send a BIFF letter responding firmly to that.

Should You Send a Copy to Anyone Else?

Often, people are tempted to send a copy of an email or letter to other people who may or may not be involved. In the above case, the Disgruntled Client mentioned that his wife and his attorney agreed with him. The mediator considered sending his BIFF to her and to his attorney, but realized that it would be more likely to make the issue grow larger, rather than grow smaller. The wife and the attorney would have asked the client questions about the letters, the client probably would have felt defensive since his request was rejected, and he may have escalated his attacks against the mediator.

The mediator also considered whether the client's attorney would believe his client and develop a negative opinion of the mediator. Since the attorney only had his client's distorted information, the mediator thought about correcting any misimpressions his attorney may have had. However, he had not indicated in his letter that he had sent a copy to anyone, so that the mediator did not need to send a copy in response.

In Chapter Two I suggested that a copy of any BIFF response should be sent to the same people who received the initial Blamespeak communication. However, if you don't know whether it has been sent to anyone else, it often is a good idea to keep your response on a small scale rather than making it into a larger scale.

I have also learned over the years that many HCPs exaggerate to make themselves feel more powerful. They often say that other people totally agree with them, when they have never even spoken to them about it. They make assumptions or totally fabricate conversations. Therefore, if the person didn't indicate that a copy was sent to anyone else, I suggest that you leave other people out of it. The general principle here is: Make it small, rather than being the one to make it big.

The mediator also realized that if the attorney believed what this client said about the mediator, then it was unlikely that he would change his mind. In general, most *reasonable* people don't jump to conclusions about other people based on one *high-conflict* person's statement.

The mediator also knew that most HCPs eventually blame their other professionals and business associates the same way that this client was blaming the mediator. So his attorney would find out sooner or later that his client was an HCP, and nothing further needed to be done to make that point. Most HCPs make themselves known eventually, as they attack each person who tries to help them.

A High-Conflict Business Partner Example

James is one of four partners who own a video production company. They mostly work on their own projects, but share space, equipment and office management, including billing and expenses. They have shared clerical and accounting staff, but for the past three years James has been the manager of the office and staff – the managing partner.

One of the other partners, Mike, appears to have a high-conflict personality, as he regularly yells at the staff and bad-mouths James to people in the community. James has spoken to Mike about some of these concerns, and Mike always brushes it off as stress and just an isolated incident. "Sure, sure," he says. "Don't worry so much. Not a problem."

The other partners like to avoid conflict. They agree Mike can be a problem sometimes and tell James to deal with him, as the managing partner. Mike seems to see James as a target of blame, so the other partners are able to mostly ignore his outbursts.

James has consulted a conflict coach and has decided to put his concerns in writing. Here is his first draft. Is this a BIFF? Would this trigger defensiveness or change in Mike?

> Dear Mike,
>
> As you know, for the last three years you and the other partners have asked me to manage the office. I have worked hard to make this an efficient and friendly place to work. However, there are some problems that keep coming up with your behavior that need to be seriously addressed. I have tried to discuss them with you, but you usually make little of them and nothing changes.
>
> I am getting more feedback from the office staff about interactions with you that are causing increasing concern. You need to develop a more positive attitude, to make things better for our staff, to make a better impression on our clients and to bring us more success in our business.
>
> Here is a list of the issues that need your attention. Some we have previously discussed and others have arisen more recently.
>
> 1. Do not treat anyone with disrespect. This has been especially a problem with how you treat the office staff. Your disrespectful manner is unhelpful and hurts morale. A good example is how you

sometimes yell out "You're doing it all wrong! You don't know what you're doing!" Or: "Our business can't survive. I work with a bunch of incompetents." You sometimes yell that at staff and sometimes at your clients. Other clients can overhear you.

2. Do not discuss office procedures with the staff. Discuss them with me. No changes of procedure will occur without a decision from me. Remember, my role is to manage the office. Please do not interfere. Come to me with any proposed changes of procedure.

3. Do not take blank checks from the office. Remember, I am the managing partner and I have been signing checks for the past three years. While you are technically on the account, it seriously interferes with our bookkeeping to have you make your own deposits and write and sign checks. If something is a rush, make sure to bring it to my attention and I will deal with it.

4. Do not use Studio B on the weekends with your clients. We have discussed this several times. I meet there with my students. When we come in and you are using Studio B, I have to rearrange the set-up and equipment. We have discussed this several times and you have always agreed. "Sure, sure," you say. "No problem." But then it still is a problem.

5. Do not talk to my clients if you are going to criticize my work. I heard you telling one of them that they should switch to you, because you could do the job so much better. This is totally inappropriate.

Do not talk about me in negative terms in the community. I have been told by others that you have said things like: "James is an a-hole." "They're all a bunch of incompetents." "They're working in the dark ages of videography." You must stop this disrespectful practice immediately. This will hurt all of us.

For the past three years I have received a slightly higher percentage of our revenues to compensate me for serving as the managing partner. However, I am concerned that you are taking advantage of this arrangement by disrespecting my efforts and creating more work for me. I have tried to be respectful of you and your special concerns from time to time. However, you must stop this abuse of me and the staff. It is unwarranted and makes it less desirable to work here. Please make every effort to develop a positive attitude from now on. I am hopeful that you will do so and that we will all benefit as we work together.

Sincerely,

James

Managing Partner

Is it a BIFF?

Brief? No. Sometimes you need to address several issues at once, so that a business BIFF may be longer than many of the BIFFs earlier in this book. However, I believe this one needs to be much shorter. If Mike is an HCP (and he sounds like one if he has these outbursts and talks negatively in public about James), then this will trigger his HCP defensiveness. It needs to be re-worded and much shorter. So, no. It's not brief, so it's not a BIFF.

Informative? No. It's informative in terms of telling Mike what he should stop doing, which is negative feedback (see next section below). But it's not informative in the friendly, neutral language intended by BIFF responses. To have any chance of success with an HCP, the information needs to be focused on something positive, friendly, and future-focused – such as what James' vision of successful interactions looks like.

Friendly? No. A list of "do nots" will trigger almost anyone's defensiveness, HCP or not. This would not feel friendly, especially to an HCP. A friendly response provides encouraging words, optimism that problems can be solved, and a sense of connection between the writer and the reader. Even though the last two sentences are positive and hopeful, all of the prior sentences heavily outweigh them.

Firm? No. While this letter spells out many problems, it just says to stop engaging in negative behaviors, rather than suggesting positive behaviors and/or deadlines for change. At the end James just says: "Please make every effort to develop a positive attitude from now on. I am hopeful that you will do so and that we will all benefit as we work together." While this is friendly, it could include clearer expectations in order to be firm and helpful to Mike.

Let's look at what he ended up writing after his consultation with a conflict coach:

> Dear Mike,
>
> I have always appreciated your passion for videography. You have had more years in this career and I still learn from you each year. I respect your commitment to learning and growing. I know I probably have not said that enough over the years.
>
> Over the past few months I have written you letters and we have had formal meetings on issues regarding specific problems that remain unresolved and need immediate attention:
>
> 1. You have at times been very loud, demeaning and aggressive with the office staff. You need to use a normal level conversational voice with them and simply make requests. They will listen to your requests and consider them.
>
> 2. You need to follow the terms of our office management agreement, including allowing me (or the staff at my direction) to make all deposits, sign all checks, make any policy changes (but

your suggestions are always welcome), and check with me before you use Studio B on Saturdays. If you have concerns or disagreements, please come to me – I will consider and respect any of your ideas.

3. You need to avoid making negative statements about me in the community. Write it down if you need to vent, or tell me directly. You acknowledged this difficulty in our last meeting and said you would try to be more careful, so I have hopes that you recognize this is a problem and will stop it immediately.

I have been patient with these problems in the past, but now things really need to improve. If they do not improve immediately in the above three areas, then I will request that you attend at least six counseling sessions with a mutually agreed-upon mental health practitioner. If you are unable to fulfill this request, then I will ask you to wind down and end your interest in this partnership. I hope this won't be necessary. My strong preference is for us to continue to work together, with mutual respect and joy in our work. Please let me know if you have questions about any of this.

Sincerely,

James

Is it a BIFF?

Brief? Yes. It is relatively short given its purpose. It focuses briefly on only three issues (instead of the previous six) and specific consequences if change doesn't happen.

Informative? Yes. James describes some of the undesired behaviors, but puts the emphasis on informing Mike of some of the desired alternate behaviors.

Friendly? Yes. James wants them to be able to keep working together, so he makes this clear. He mentions how he respects Mike's skills and hopes things can work out. This is important, so that the message of hope is stronger than the message about problems needing change.

Firm? Yes. In this case, James has described the needed behavior changes, *and* consequences if they don't occur – counseling or ending his role in the partnership. There's nothing further to discuss or negotiate. All of Mike's energy needs to go into making changes, not arguing about the past. James has made this possible, by putting the focus on the future.

Should You Avoid Negative Feedback?

When someone has acted badly, as Mike did in this case, isn't it better to emphasize how bad he has been? Shouldn't we really point this out to him, so that he "gets" it? Aren't you just rewarding his bad behavior by mostly ignoring it? These are all common misunderstandings when it comes to dealing with HCPs. The problem is a lack of self-management skills.

Remember, they don't "get" the effect of their own behavior on others. Remember, they have a hidden psychological barrier to self-awareness and self-change. Trying to make them "get it" will only trigger more defensiveness.

You're not rewarding bad behavior; you are just focusing on teaching a better behavior. Criticizing the past when people don't have the skills will get you nowhere – perhaps you have already experienced this in dealing with a high-conflict person.

Therefore, with HCPs it helps to avoid "negative feedback," which commonly has three negative ingredients that make it unhelpful:

1. It tends to focus on the whole person. "You should be ashamed of your*self*." "You'll never get it right." "You are a disgrace." This is all-or-nothing thinking. While these types of comments are often made to motivate people to behave more reasonably, the effect it usually has is to trigger extreme defensiveness and an angry attack back. Remember, HCPs are lacking in the skills you want, so that trying to motivate them with disparaging remarks will not make them suddenly have skills.

2. It tends to include a harshly negative tone of voice. Tone of voice is one of the triggers for HCPs. They are highly sensitive to whether you are going to be yet another person who criticizes them, as they have

received criticism all their lives. It's much more successful to give them an encouraging tone of voice that communicates empathy and respect. These may be the needed words to get the HCP to try something new.

3. It tends to stay focused on the past. Sometimes you need to make comments or decisions based on past behavior. However, if you are going to remain in a business or professional relationship with the person, it is best to shift the focus to the future and *how* to make needed changes. HCPs are often stuck in the present moment and defending themselves, so it may take a while to shift them to learning new skills. Yet that is the goal.

Keeping these aspects of negative feedback in mind helps us understand the importance of focusing on the future and strengthening positive skills. HCPs often have positive skills – they just need to have them reinforced to make them work. In the above example, if Mike does not have the skills, so that his difficult behavior continues, then practicing new skills with a counselor for six sessions is a good solution. It puts the emphasis on learning skills for the future. A positive future focus is always more effective with HCPs, whether it's in business, professional work or anywhere.

A Public Relations Example

A few years ago two pizza employees made a video of themselves sticking cheese up their noses and putting it on food they were preparing to deliver, and other pranks.

It went viral and lots of people had a big laugh. I don't know whether the two employees were HCPs, but there were reports that one had a criminal history (which might indicate a *pattern* of high-conflict behavior), and they certainly had very bad judgment that affected the whole business. Did they think that people would believe that they were actually doing this, or just faking it? Apparently they were truly surprised when their employer found out!

Many people lost their faith in the company and sales started to plummet. The pizza company realized how important it was to provide a quick response. They developed and implemented a social media campaign and posted a video on YouTube featuring the company president that was just under two minutes, including the following statements:

> This was an isolated incident... There is nothing more important or sacred to us than our customers' trust... It sickens me that the acts of two individuals could impact our great system.

Is it a BIFF?

Brief? Yes. It was just under two minutes and probably the perfect length for addressing this problem to the public.

Informative? Yes. It explained the actions the company was taking to clean up the store, to tighten hiring procedures and to immediately fire and bring legal action against the two employees. The focus was the key points above: that it was an isolated incident, their customers are "sacred" to them and that they are still a great company.

Friendly? Yes, toward their customers. It was understandable that they were not friendly toward the two fired employees, but they didn't get stuck on blasting them – they kept the focus on what the company was doing.

Firm? Yes. They made it clear that the problem was small and had been resolved.

This is a good example of taking a rumor seriously and giving a quick response. Apparently the company totally recovered. It demonstrates the importance of quick BIFFs in today's interconnected world for any business, organization or individual.

High-Conflict Opinions Are Contagious

Brain research has shown that emotions are contagious – positive and negative. The more intense the emotion, the more contagious it is. This helps us survive as a group with quick action when needed. We are an incredible wireless network for emotions. Intense fear, anger, laughter, sadness, and all the other emotions can ripple through a group much faster than logical thought.

I believe that this is because our right brains think faster and pay more attention to non-verbal cues – such as the expressions on other people's faces when something awful and/or funny is happening. We automatically trust the emotions of a group in the absence of opposing emotions or credible information. In fact, we seem to believe emotional opinions without bothering to logically examine the situation. "Since so many people believe it, I believe it!"

Perhaps this is because we are social beings with a long history of communicating by emotions for thousands of years before we learned to read and write and scientifically analyze information. In addition, the amygdalas in the middle of our brains act like smoke alarms. In the face of alarming information, they shut down our slow, logical thought processes.

So alarming information travels quickly and widely – and shuts down logical thought for many people. When the pizza company executives thought that no one would take the video seriously, I think they were counting on people using their left brains to analyze the situation. Unfortunately, people don't work that way. They simply adopted the intensely widespread opinion that this pizza company was out of control of its employees – and stopped buying their pizza. Today, opinions can be fast, emotional and widespread.

The result is that businesses everywhere must be prepared to respond quickly whenever there is negative news about them. Otherwise, it may be swallowed whole by a public that is tuned in to everyone else's opinions – in an emotional, repetitive and alarming manner.

Conclusion

Businesses and professionals have similar issues. They often are dealing with people who look and sound good, but are not what they seemed at first. Rather than get angry at them, it helps to write or say BIFFs that focus on the positive aspects of the present relationship, while also informing the HCP about what changes are needed and what the consequences are if they do not change.

It's hard to shift focus from giving negative feedback to HCPs to giving friendly BIFFs, but you will find that it is possible and has better results – especially with practice. If some feedback about the past is necessary, you can still keep the emphasis on what to do in the future. If HCPs or anyone has put you in a bad position in public, you can use BIFFs to quickly provide accurate, verifiable information. In business and the professions, future positive relationships – private and public – are essential to all of your future work.

CHAPTER EIGHT

Organizations and Governments

Most of us have been or will be involved in several organizations, whether a neighborhood committee, a parent-teacher association, a church or other religious membership, volunteer work, political parties, athletic, educational or otherwise. Such organizations attract HCPs, because they usually welcome almost anyone who shares their interests. Members of many of these organizations are not screened for conflict resolution skills or any other skills.

Such organizations also have rules and procedures. HCPs are often the ones who won't follow the rules and procedures, or who want to get into positions of power so that they can try to impose their own rules and procedures on others. Most of these types of organizations encourage members to take leadership roles, so that they are more vulnerable to the quick rise of individuals who have these problems.

This is not to say that volunteer leaders and others are all HCPs – most are not. This is just to say that HCPs can more easily slip through the cracks and into leadership roles in these types of organizations than they would in business or the professions. (They show up there as well, as described in the previous chapter. It just takes them a little more work to get there.)

Religious organizations particularly struggle with how to handle HCPs, because they value every individual, their procedures are slow and forgiving, and the membership becomes divided over what to do. When a religious leader is an HCP, it can be confusing to determine whether the conflicts are over religious differences or the leader's high-conflict personality – or both.

Government agencies and employees are focused on rules and procedures, and enforcing them in society. Much of their work is dealing with HCPs who do not comply. HCPs can also get into positions of power in government agencies, because they like having power over others. However, just as with the organizations described above, this does not mean that most government workers are HCPs or that most people who use government services are HCPs – they are not. This just means that there is an attraction to HCPs, because government offers so many opportunities to receive help, or to have power and control over others.

This chapter focuses on how to present limit-setting information to uncooperative community members. The examples in this chapter can be adapted for any organization or government agency.

A High-Conflict Volunteer Example

Rosie liked to volunteer. However, she started implying to newcomers that she was on the staff. She liked to call new volunteers at all times of the day and night, to get them to take on tasks that they hadn't volunteered for. One day she became belligerent with a volunteer and told him he wasn't the right type for this organization and that he should stop being involved. He talked to the Director and complained about her, with a detailed explanation of what she had said to him to get him involved, and then what she had said to him to get him to quit. The Director of the organization decided to meet with her, but also to give her a letter explaining her narrow role, in case she didn't remember what he told her.

Dear Rosie,

We appreciate your commitment to our animal rescue program. We want to thank you for the volunteer work you have done. Our organization must maintain its high reputation in this community by following clear procedures and roles. We're sure you understand.

Therefore, it will be important from now on for you to work with Joe, as the staff member in charge of volunteers. You will need to schedule your volunteer time and tasks with him. It is very important that you do not say or imply to other volunteers that you are on the staff. I know it can be confusing when we rely on volunteers so much, but we must maintain our clear roles so that our funding sources and the community knows what to expect and how we are operating.

Please let me know if you have any questions.

Best Wishes!

Daniel

Is This a BIFF?

Brief?
Informative?
Friendly?
Firm?

You can decide. You'll recognize similarities with the examples in the prior chapter, especially the business partner example. The emphasis is on the future and what she should do, rather than the past and what she did wrong. There is no mention of consequences in this letter, as this is the first effort to "contain" her behavior. If the problem continues, she can be informed about consequences or just told to leave. Maintaining her in a limited role will help keep her from stirring up trouble outside of the organization if she was kicked out right away. HCPs have a way of making volunteer organizations suffer when they feel slighted. This appears to be because expectations are so high and anyone is allowed to be a member. This is very attractive to HCPs, who want to help but have a hard time fitting in somewhere. When there are clear tasks and boundaries, many HCPs do very well in a wide range of organizations.

Should One Person Deal With an HCP?

HCPs often bring a lot of complaints to various non-governmental organizations and government agencies, because they believe they are victims so much of the time. Many organizations and agencies have personnel and procedures for processing complaints. Many have started to see a pattern of complainants who keep coming back, talking to different people each time. HCPs are good at finding the cracks in procedures and the splits in philosophy of organizations and agencies.

This leads to different staff dealing with them differently and often undermining the limit-setting of prior staff members. This can result in burn-out and create chaos in organizations and agencies. Therefore, one solution is to have one person that complainants or returning complainants deal with, so that there won't be undermining or confusion about what was said and done before. It's important to give this person a break after 6-12 months in that role. This approach can help in any organization, government agency or business, so that when a potential HCP is identified, one person can be assigned to deal with them.

A City Code Enforcement Example

This BIFF is an example of sending a letter in response to *inaction* by a possible HCP, rather than in response to a communication from an HCP. Since HCPs generally like to deal with problems on their own terms, or avoid the rules and regulations of those in authority positions, there are many situations like this that arise for organizations or governments. See if you think the following is a BIFF response to a potentially high-conflict situation.

Letter to Home Owner

(There should be an attempt to meet in person, but this letter can be left if no response.)

Dear Mr/Ms Smith:

I came to your house today to meet you as one of our home owners in Oak Park. We are proud of our community and we are especially proud of working together with citizens to solve problems. One of the problems that comes up from time to time, is when a lot of building materials get left in a yard for a long time. This can lead to risks of children getting injured, fires simmering, and lowered property values for everyone. Often property owners just lose track of how much time has passed when they are working on their homes and need a reminder to clean up the materials.

We have noticed a large amount of materials building up in your yard for quite a while. We would like to work with you on solving this problem. The city code requires us to give you a Notice of a Violation if action isn't taken in a reasonable time period. We want to give you a chance to clean up your yard without a Notice of Violation. If you can give us a reasonable date by which you will do that, we can avoid the Notice at this time.

Please give me a call at the phone number above if you want to discuss this. If we don't hear from you within seven days of the date on this letter, we will need to take further action without your input. I hope that won't be necessary and that we can solve this together. You can give me a phone call or write to me at the address above with your intended cleanup date and I'll let you know if it works for us. Thanks.

Sincerely,

Margaret Hall, Officer

Municipal Code Enforcement

Is This a BIFF?

Brief? 1-3 paragraphs (one page) are the most any letter like this should be. Too much triggers a defensive response.

Informative? This focuses on factual information. It doesn't include any opinions, threats, or disrespectful comments. It avoids the 3 A's: Admonishments, Advice and Apologies.

Friendly? It starts and ends with friendly phrases: "I wanted to meet you." "You're a property owner." "You may have lost track of time." "Let's work together on this." She also gave a choice of how to respond and a choice of a cleanup date.

Firm? A deadline was given, so action will occur whether the owner participates or not. She informed the owner that a Notice of Violation was a consequence, and she wanted to help the owner avoid that.

The Need to Set Limits with HCPs

You may have noticed that I suggested not to make threats, but then I said it's useful to inform about possible consequences – also known as setting limits. The difference is that threats are intended to be *threatening*, whereas informing about consequences can be done by someone who intends to be *helpful*. They are both forms of setting limits, but informing about consequences seems to be much more effective with HCPs.

Threats are usually made in a hostile manner and are often about being against each other in a relationship, such as:

> If you don't stop doing 'A,' then I'm going to do 'B!'

> If you don't do 'X,' then I'm not going to work with you anymore.

> If you continue to leave materials out in a dangerous manner, then I'll serve you with a Notice of Violation.

It doesn't take much to hear the threatening tone in all of these. HCPs certainly hear it.

Instead, you can feel the difference when someone says:

> You may not realize this, but if you do 'A,' then our department is required to do 'B.'

The city code requires us to give you a Notice of Violation if action isn't taken in a reasonable time period.

We want to give you a chance to clean up your yard without a Notice of Violation.

If you can give us a reasonable date by which you will do that, we can avoid the Notice at this time.

The last four are examples of *us against the problem* rather than us against each other. They are a form of *indirect confrontation*, like those described in Chapter 6. If you present consequences as neutral information, with a friendly introductory phrase like those used in the letter above, then they are likely to be considered more thoughtfully. If your goal is to vent your frustration, then threats feel good to you for a few minutes, but they trigger HCP defensiveness. If your goal is to solve a problem, then *informing about consequences* in a *friendly manner* is a much better way to go and more likely to help HCPs focus on problem-solving in a calm manner. After all, a sense of calm, contentment and safety is associated with the left hemisphere of the brain, whereas fear and anger are associated with the right brain.

Giving Two Choices

One form of setting limits is to give people two choices and inform them about their related consequences. This can be especially helpful in crisis situations. It can focus people's attention on *thinking logically* about these two choices, rather than having them feel defensive about having no choice at all or feeling overwhelmed by having too many choices. My favorite way of presenting this is to say:

> You have two choices: The easy way or the hard way. The easy way is to stop yelling, sit down and wait your turn. The hard way is to keep yelling and I will call security. You will get your turn faster doing it the easy way.

This approach doesn't just threaten them – it gives them a sense of choice, limited as it is. It puts the burden on the person to decide. It shows that you are respecting their right to make this decision. Of course, if the HCP doesn't or can't decide because she is too flooded emotionally, that is itself a decision that you will need to use the "hard way" consequences.

A Law Enforcement Example

Law enforcement officers have to deal with some of the most high-conflict people, during some of their most high-conflict moments. Yet they can use BIFFs to keep HCPs calm in some cases. Giving two choices is often a way of doing this. For example, when a police officer is on the scene dealing with a probable HCP who is losing control (possibly drunk), he could say:

> I want to help you. You can leave with me now voluntarily, or I can arrest you for disturbing the peace. It's your choice. But those are the only two

options I'm allowed to give you right now. You have five seconds to decide.

Is it a BIFF?

Brief? Yes, so long as there's time to give a choice. Sometimes there has to be instant action without any choices. But HCPs often escalate for a while before they lose control.

Informative? Yes. It informs the person of the two choices and that the officer is limited to those two options in this situation – a form of indirect confrontation.

Friendly? Yes. The officer has said he'd like to help the person, as a way of introducing these two choices.

Firm? Yes. There's only two choices presented, and five seconds for the person to make the choice.

Of course, sometimes there's no choice. The decision has already been made. For example, I once saw the following situation unfold when a police officer had to remove an uncooperative person from an airplane (before it took off):

Officer: You have to come with me.

Fred: No. I have a right to be here.

Officer: Oh, that's already been decided. What's your first
           name?

Fred: Fred.

Officer: Okay, Fred. Are these your belongings?

Fred: Yes.

Officer: Okay, Fred, I'll help you gather those.

Fred: But I'm not going anywhere.

Officer: Oh, that's already been decided. Here, I'll take
           these items and you can take those.

The officer picked up some of his items and started moving away with them – and Fred followed peacefully!

It was amazing how the officer just moved Fred along, with *Brief* questions and comments, *Informing* him as he went, in a *Friendly* and *Firm* manner. He stayed matter of fact and the possible HCP stopped resisting him and cooperated.

Of course, the officer carried himself in a manner that said he could easily take Fred against his will if necessary, and there was another officer available out of sight if force was necessary. He just made it unnecessary in this case.

Conclusion

This is a brief chapter for a wide category of potential HCP problems. But the BIFFs described above can be used in most organizations and by most government agencies. Often the situation for organizations or government agencies is one in which there has been no action or there has been bad behavior directed at others. In these cases, it is important to explain rules and procedures – with consequences – in a friendly manner that has both of you working together against the problem.

Setting deadlines is also very appropriate and usually necessary with HCPs, if earlier discussions of the problem have had no impact. This should still be done in a friendly manner.

In general, one of the problems in today's society with HCPs is that most people tend to use negative comments instead of consequences to motivate them to change their negative behavior. With HCPs we need to use positive comments combined with firm consequences. This is more likely to motivate them to cooperate.

In today's world, an increasing number of people believe that they can challenge or attack people in positions of authority. For HCPs, large organizations and government agencies are easy targets of blame – they expect that you will have to listen and treat them nicely as they complain. Rather than get defensive about it, just give them a BIFF.

CHAPTER NINE

Politicians

Politicians are among those who use Blamespeak the most –
because it often works for them! In recent elections people
have deplored the use of negative ads, yet they have been
used more than ever. They grab your attention and make
you concerned. While most politicians in the past were not
HCPs, the times we live in seem to reinforce and encourage
high-conflict politicians. In our highly competitive world of
news, the most extreme behavior gets the most attention.

The effect of this trend will be more and more high-
conflict politicians getting elected – and acting badly. Those
who live by Blamespeak will often crash by Blamespeak –
and we have seen many politicians getting pushed out of
office for bad behavior in recent years. High-conflict people
have predictable patterns of behavior – at least to those who
pay attention to HCP dynamics.

HCPs in politics often start out by alleging to be heroes
against evil villains – an all-or-nothing approach. "Elect me
and I will eliminate the fraud and corruption of the prior
government official." The ones who say this the loudest are

often the HCPs, because they rely on extreme emotions to hook in the electorate and often promise extreme solutions.

But government is a messy and flexible business. It has to somehow deal with differences of opinions in ways that everyone can tolerate. Good politicians can get work done by managing these differences, with respect for everyone, including people who hold opposite points of view. High-conflict politicians are less able to manage differences and resort to all-or-nothing thinking, exaggerated emotions and extreme solutions – which they claim that they alone know how to accomplish! Beware!

The "Issue" is Not the Issue

This chapter includes two examples of possible BIFFs in response to real statements – one by a Democrat and one by a Republican. No names are mentioned, as the point is to practice how to respond, not how to judge or promote one party or another. There are plenty of HCPs in all parties, for the same reasons that there are plenty of HCPs in all the other settings described in this book: HCPs seem to be increasing in society and they are attracted to conflict where they can get attention and thrive.

HCPs make it look like there is a legal or political issue, but often the "issue" is not the issue – their personality is the issue. In the following two examples, I don't know if anyone was an HCP and my facts are certainly not complete. I never met the people involved and there are always many points of view about politicians. What is important here are the concepts of how to respond to political Blamespeak.

A City Politician

News reports indicated that the city attorney, who repre-
sented the city in legal matters, wrote a public letter to the
mayor accusing him of fraud by saying the mayor had
made "false and misleading statements" about the city's
pension plan. This was a serious matter, because there
were some investigations going on about whether some
politicians had participated in criminal acts regarding
pension decisions prior to the mayor's term in office.

However, the city attorney had a reputation for filing
and losing lawsuits relating to city business and financial
decisions. Apparently the legal bill for outside lawyers
working on all of these lawsuits was over $3.5 million,
whereas the prior city attorney's outside use of lawyers was
only around $100,000.

He never produced any credible evidence that the
mayor had committed fraud, but news reports said there
was a "civil war" going on between them. Apparently,
the mayor got emotionally hooked one day and angrily told
the city attorney in public to, "Look in the mirror!" This just
made things worse and reinforced the civil war perception.
This often happens if you use counter-Blamespeak, as
I described in the first chapter of this book.

Interestingly, a news analyst eventually suggested that
the issue's not the issue: "And while people say the war
should stop, the conflict over the role of the city attorney –
and [his] own personality – practically guarantees there
will be more clashes."

What should the mayor have done? Should he have
ignored the allegations of fraud against him made publicly
by the city attorney? My view, as described in Chapter Two,

is that you need to respond in the same format when there is credible misinformation being spread to others about or against you – otherwise it may be accepted as true. If someone publicly accuses you of fraud and it's a current issue in the public, but there's no evidence of it having anything to do with you, then I think you should say something like this at the next public opportunity:

> I appreciate the city attorney's concern about the city's finances. We are in a very hard situation and I share those concerns. Several auditors have looked into decisions that were made over the years affecting our finances – decisions that I was not involved in – and none of them have reached the conclusion that they were fraudulent or criminal. I believe that none of us should use these extreme terms no matter how upset we are, unless there is evidence to back them up. I know that the city attorney wants the best for our city, so I suggest we focus now on the future rather than the past. I know that's what I'm going to do.

Is it a BIFF?

Brief? For a politician, that is very brief and all that's necessary.

Informative? It informs the public that there is no basis to any allegations against the mayor.

Friendly? The mayor said he shared the city attorney's concerns and said he knew that the city attorney wanted the best for the city. Given that he had been publicly accused of fraud, these words are very generous.

Firm? The mayor has closed the door on the issue by suggesting that they both focus on the future.

After that type of statement, the mayor doesn't need to respond again. In this case, I believe that the mayor simply ignored the statement and things simmered until other public matters distracted them both. The mayor avoided getting emotionally hooked by future comments against him by the city attorney, who accused so many public officials of so many things that he lost most of his credibility by the time he sought re-election. The election results: the city attorney lost by nearly 60%-40% – a significant defeat for any politician, especially one who saw himself as a popular hero against all the villains. And the mayor *won* re-election by a similar large margin.

Quickly Inform the Potential Negative Advocates

Just as in the business public relations example in Chapter Eight, it is very important to respond to Blamespeak quickly with factual information in politics. The reason for this is that high-conflict emotions and opinions are highly contagious. The public absorbs the feeling of alarm, especially when it is repeated over and over again in the same highly emotional manner by the media involved.

Brain research shows that when people are anxious is when they are most likely to absorb other people's emotions. This may explain some mob behavior. The amygdalas in our brains, as I explained in Chapter Three, are particularly reactive to facial expressions of fear and anger, which often get played over and over again on television and the Internet. This alarm system shuts down logical thinking, in order to focus all of our energy on quick defensive reactions.

This means that you cannot let misinformation or drama overcome your useful and factual information. Since high-conflict emotions and opinions are passed on to others in an automatic and unconscious brain process, you need to act quickly to inform people who may be reacting to the "alarm" without logical problem-solving.

Speak up and explain your point of view in a BIFF manner as quickly as possible. Otherwise, many people will become Negative Advocates for the HCP politician and their point of view will not allow yours to enter their minds weeks or months (or even days) later. Once you are solidified as the enemy and someone to fear, it is a lot harder to get people to listen to you with an open mind.

Remember, people don't logically analyze situations once they have become emotionally alarmed and convinced there is a terrible crisis. They follow their emotional leader, especially one who presents a point of view with certainty and confidence (even when he or she is completely wrong!).

Make sure you are not angry with an HCP's Negative Advocates. They are emotionally hooked and uninformed. Educate them with factual information and your own empathy for their concerns, with BIFF types of messages.

A National Politician

In an interview, soon after he won an election, a national politician said that the current president, who he mentioned by name, was "one of the most corrupt presidents in modern times." Should the President respond to this statement?

In contrast to the city attorney, there was no public concern that anyone near the president had committed fraud and there were no fraud investigations going on. So when a newly elected politician makes a broad, non-specific statement, it is generally viewed as someone still campaigning and can be ignored.

However, if he had made a specific allegation against the president, a response may have been necessary. Ideally, responding to outrageous statements at the national level is something the news media should do – by asking questions.

In this case, a few days later this politician backed down some and said that the President was "not personally corrupt." He later backed down further and clarified that he believed the president was engaging in "business as usual," as both parties had done in the past. In other words, the statement about the most corrupt president had nothing actually to do with corruption, but simply different points of view. Unfortunately, a lot of people can get emotionally hooked by such language, as it triggers their deep sense of danger – and future logical information on the subject may not get through.

But what if there was an investigation going on at the time related to national finances? How should a politician who was not involved respond? The same way as the BIFF described above for the mayor:

"I appreciate the official's concern about the nation's finances. We are in a very hard situation and I share those concerns. Several investigations have looked into decisions that were made over the years affecting our finances – decisions that I was not involved in – and none of them have reached the conclusion that they were fraudulent or criminal. I believe that none of us should use these extreme terms no matter how upset we are, unless there is evidence to back them up. I know that this official wants the best for our country, so I suggest we focus now on the future rather than the past. I know that's what I'm going to do."

And that's it: BIFF.

Don't Make it Personal

For the reasons above, it is important not to make your BIFFs personal in public in politics. Try to avoid using the potentially high-conflict person's name in your public BIFFs. Instead, refer to the "concerns" that have been raised and address those concerns. Firmly state your principles and explain your decisions. Avoid reacting to the HCPs bad behavior and using judgmental words about it in public. Otherwise, you look like a bully and the HCP can organize his or her Negative Advocates against what you just said.

You can accomplish the same goal by discussing concerns and principles. You will get credit for "taking the high road" if you can do that in the heat of political battles. No one's perfect and you will make mistakes, but if you went into politics to make the world a better place BIFFs give you a chance to do that.

Conclusion

Whether you're running for office as the class president at your school, or in a local government, or at the national level, BIFFs may earn you credibility and help you stand out in today's political Culture of Blame and Disrespect. When you are able to restrain yourself and calmly (but firmly) respond, people may see you as someone they can trust to handle conflicts and crises better than an HCP.

Unfortunately, Blamespeak in politics works – in the short run. It gets attention for HCPs who want attention more than anything else. But it doesn't work in the long run. If you can pace yourself and restrain the urge to use Blamespeak and counter-Blamespeak, you may have a lasting and successful political career.

CHAPTER TEN

Coaching for BIFF Responses

Now that you know how to write a BIFF response, let's address coaching for BIFF responses. It's always a good idea to show your BIFF response to someone else before you send it. That person's feedback may save you a lot of headaches by catching any sentences that may be too inflammatory, long-winded or defensive. It helps to get feedback from someone who is good at being a BIFF coach.

You also may be asked to be a BIFF coach for your friends and family members, or you may be a professional coach who wants to add BIFF response coaching to your services. This chapter spells out a very simple method we have developed for coaching for BIFF responses. Since High Conflict Institute was established several years ago, we have coached dozens of business partners, human resource professionals, neighbors, parents of adult children, spouses going through a divorce, and many others. We've learned that coaching for BIFF responses can be highly effective if the coach asks the following ten questions of the individual who has written a draft of a BIFF Response (who I'll call the "client" – whether it's a business client, friend or family member).

---

1. Is it Brief?
2. Is it Informative?
3. Is it Friendly?
4. Is it Firm?
5. Does it contain any Advice?
6. Does it contain any Admonishments?
7. Does it contain any Apologies?
8. How do you think the other person will respond?
9. Is there anything you would take out, add or change?
10. Would you like to hear my thoughts about it?

The Goal of Coaching for a BIFF Response

To be most helpful, a coach for a BIFF response should point out that there is no single "right" way to write a BIFF response. In many ways it's like cooking. What works for one person is almost always different from what works for another person. The BIFF response always belongs to the person writing it. It is very important for the BIFF coach to avoid "correcting" the client's BIFF response as soon as it has been written. The goal is to help the client *learn to write* BIFF responses, so she can do them on her own in the future, if necessary. The only way to effectively do that is to help the client *analyze her own* BIFF response. These questions keep the focus on helping the client do just that.

You will notice that the very last question is *"Would you like to hear my thoughts about it?"* You might wonder why that isn't the first question. You might really, really want to give suggestions right away. But by keeping this question for last, you put the focus on having the client really think about what he has written. This means that when you ask the first question, *"Is it Brief?"* you are careful not to start suggesting how it could be longer or shorter. Let the person think about it for a moment and decide for himself. That way, it keeps the focus on the Client's own analysis and strengthens his learning of this skill to use on his own.

Introducing the 10 Questions

You can introduce the 10 Questions with an explanation like this:

> "Whenever we write a BIFF response, it helps to discuss it with someone else before we send it. When I've given my BIFF drafts to someone else, they have usually suggested that I trim them down – sometimes even cutting them in half! And I've usually agreed! It's hard to see in our own comments what might trigger more anger or misbehavior from the other person. It's often easier for someone else to spot those trigger words or sentences. But I want to start out by letting you analyze your BIFF response, as this will help you get better and better at writing BIFFs that accomplish what you want.

"So I would like you to read your BIFF out loud. Then, I'm going to help you by asking you 10 questions, so you can think about your BIFF. And remember, there's no one right way of writing a BIFF. It depends on three things: Who's writing the BIFF response, who's receiving it and what the situation is. So my goal is to help you think about whether it will accomplish what *you* want with the person *you* are dealing with at this time."

BIFF Writers Feel Vulnerable

One thing we have learned about coaching BIFF clients is that they often feel very vulnerable, because they are usually dealing with a high-conflict person (an HCP) who is criticizing them mercilessly or making the their lives miserable in some other way. When your clients write BIFF responses, they are trying to regain a sense of balance and peace, so it is a time when they are very vulnerable to the feedback of others. Therefore, it is very important that they feel safe with you, rather than detect even a hint of personal criticism, as you help them decide whether they believe it's going to be an effective BIFF.

With this in mind, it helps to be encouraging during the first nine questions, rather than analyzing your client's writing in detail at first. Your response to her answers can be positive, while leaving room for you to make suggestions at the end with question ten. So when your client says: "I think it's brief," you can say "Okay," or "It looks like that to me too," and move on. If she asks for your feedback right away, just say, *"Let's come back to that after you answer the ten questions first."*

You can use a similar response when the client thinks about whether it's Informative. This questioning process does not need a big response. Most often the client will simply say: "Yes, I think it is informative." Then you can say: "Ok. And do you think that it's friendly?" You can go through this questioning process quickly or slowly, depending on what the client wants to say about it.

Then, when you get to say your thoughts at the end (but only if the client says, "Yes, I want to hear your thoughts"), you can say something like this: "While it looks brief, you might want to take out the third sentence, and make it even briefer. That sentence seems like it might trigger an emotional response because of … But of course, it's up to you. It's your BIFF. What do you think about that?"

Sometimes, the client will spontaneously decide to change something. That's great! In this situation, you can ask the client what he thinks about it now. You might ask your client to read it out loud again and see what they think. Remember to keep the focus on *the client's analysis* of the BIFF – not yours.

The 3 A's

The 3 A's are: Advice, Admonishments, and Apologies, as explained in Chapter Three. If your client is not familiar with the 3 A's or has forgotten them, you can briefly explain these when you ask questions 5-7:

5. **Does it contain any Advice?** By this, I mean are you telling the other person how to deal with a particular problem a particular way? This almost always

triggers a defensive and often attacking response. Unless the person you're dealing with specifically asked for your advice, it's usually better not to give it – especially in a BIFF response that's intended to end the conversation or give two limited choices. So do you see any advice in your BIFF as it's currently written?

6. **Does it contain any Admonishments?** In other words, are you speaking to the person like a parent telling a child how to behave? This never works in a BIFF. When people are feeling defensive, the last thing they want is for you to tell them they are doing something wrong. The whole point of a BIFF is to calm yourself down and end the conversation, without triggering a defensive response. Do you see any hint of that in your BIFF as it is currently written?

7. **Does it contain any Apologies?** This can be confusing. In general, apologies are a good thing. However, if you are dealing with a high-conflict person, he may tend to use your apologies against you, like ammunition. Avoid apologizing for anything of substance, like: "I shouldn't have done such-and-such." Or: "I'm sorry I hurt you by doing xyz." Or: "I guess my strategy failed." Or: "I know I haven't been sensitive to your needs." These types of apologies blame you and HCPs are preoccupied with blame, and will use it to prove that it really is all YOUR fault! Of course, social apologies are okay, like "I'm sorry I'm a few minutes late." Or: "I'm sorry to see that you're in this difficult situation." With this in mind, do you see any apologies in what you have written?

Your Thoughts

When you finally get to question ten and your thoughts – if you have been asked to give them – it is important to make them tentative. Remember, there's no one right answer and it's up to the client to decide how it is written. For example, "You might want to think about that third sentence. I think it *might* trigger an intense response from the person you're dealing with, because he or she already said such-and-such. What do you think?"

Suppose the client says: "I agree it should be changed. How should I say it?" Ideally, you will respond by saying: "Why don't you give it a try first, and see how it sounds. You've been doing great so far." This keeps the emphasis on your goal, which is to help the client do his or her *own analysis* of the BIFF. It also helps boost the client's confidence, at a time when he may be feeling extremely vulnerable about writing anything, because of so much criticism from the person he's dealing with.

If you decide to give a suggestion, try to give two or three choices: "You might try saying… or you might try saying it this other way… What do you think?" This helps her continue to think about it and make it her own writing, rather than simply doing what you said. The best coaching is when the client feels smart, rather than feeling that the coach is brilliant. When you're coaching, it's not about you.

A School Example

Suppose your client, Sam, has written the following BIFF response draft and is ready to discuss it:

Hi Yolanda, thanks for your email. I thought about it a lot. I agree we should stop doing our math homework together. It will help us each try harder to learn it ourselves. But I disagree that I was just "using" you and not helping you at all. I'm still glad that we're friends and will talk about other things when we're together. Sam.

After you've gone through all your questions, Sam asks you for your thoughts. It could go like this:

Coach: Overall, I really like it. However, I'm concerned that the phrase 'using you' might backfire. Yolanda might focus on that and attack you back, such as: 'Well, you WERE using me. I'M the one who figured out how to really do the assignment.' Then, Sam, you'll feel even more defensive. What do you think about leaving out that phrase? Or even that whole sentence?

Sam: But I can't just let her think I was using her, because I wasn't!

Coach: Well, it's up to you, of course. But from what you've told me, I don't think you will prove anything to her on this subject. If YOU are confident that you weren't using her, then do you really need to even discuss it with her? Especially in this BIFF? Perhaps you could tell her that sometime when you are being friends talking about something else.

Sam: I'll have to think about it.

Coach: Why don't you try reading it without that third sentence, and then decide.

Sam: Ok, I'll try that. "Yolanda, thank you for your email. I thought about it a lot. I agree we should stop doing our math homework together. It will help us each try harder to learn it ourselves. I'm still glad that we're friends and will talk about other things when we're together." You're right. It does sound better that way.

Coach: Great! Let me know how it works out after you send it.

And then you can tell yourself (privately): "Way to go, Coach!"

A Community Example

Suppose your client is Charles Miller, the community manager for a Homeowners Association. He received this email from a community member:

Dear Mr. Miller,
You are insensitive, irresponsible and ignorant! You have not paid attention to the problem I told you about days ago, namely that the street light on Tennis Avenue has burned out. If you don't do something right away, I am going to bring this up at the next board meeting. You deserve to be fired!
Barry Jones

Charles calls you to be his BIFF response coach. You might start out with the following:

First of all, if you feel attacked and defensive, you are having a normal human response. However, it will make your life easier if you don't respond defensively. Instead, tell yourself that personal attacks are about the attacker, not about you. Then, try writing a BIFF response. Let me explain how that works, then you can draft a BIFF response and we can discuss it.

Then, Charles sends you the following draft BIFF response and you set up a meeting to discuss it. Here's his first try at his BIFF response:

Dear Barry,

Thank you for reminding us about the burned out bulb in the lamppost on Tennis Avenue. I passed that information on to our maintenance department on the day you told me two days ago, so there's no need to be impatient. They reported to me that they had to order the new bulb, because it is a newer design lamppost and there was a shortage of bulbs for a while. They tell me we should have it replaced within the next two days.

Sincerely,

Charles

Suppose you go through the first seven questions and he says it's Brief, Informative, Friendly and Firm, and he doesn't see any Advice, Admonishments or Apologies. You tell him he's done an amazing job for his first attempt at a BIFF response. Then, you ask him:

8. **How do you think the other person will respond?**
Charles: With the information I've given him, I think

Barry should calm down. Although I know he rarely stays calm for long.

Coach: Great!

9. **Is there anything you would take out, add or change?**
Charles: I'm wondering whether I should take out the phrase: "so there's no need to be impatient.

Coach: Try reading it out loud with the phrase, and then read it out loud without that phrase. See which one sounds better to you.

Charles (after reading it both ways out loud): It's definitely better without that phrase. He's a touchy guy and I don't want to include anything that might trigger him. What do you think?

Coach: It also sounded better to me without that phrase. But you know him better than I do and it's your BIFF. So it's up to you.

10. **Would you like to hear my thoughts about it?**
Charles: Yes. Definitely.

At this point you, as his coach, can make any suggestions, so don't hold back important ideas. But also don't overwhelm Charles with too many thoughts about it. Remember to be encouraging.

Coach: I really like it. But I think it would be even better with a nice friendly ending. How about: "We all want the community to be well lit, so thank you again for calling this to our attention. What do you think of that? Remember, it's up to you!

Charles: I like it. It gives him a pat on the back for telling me about the light a few days ago. That might help him stay calm a little longer. Sometimes he can be helpful, so why not emphasize the good stuff he does? I'm definitely going to use it. Thanks!

Conclusion

As you can see, using the 10 Questions helps the coach to focus the client on thinking about his own writing and making all the decisions about any edits. This is a good teaching tool, as it helps him remember his goal and the questions that he can ask himself if there is no coach around. He's still encouraged to ask someone to review his BIFF response, but he will also get better and better at it this way.

For you as the coach, the 10 Questions help you restrain yourself from giving too much feedback too soon. Remember, a good coach helps the client feel smart. Avoid using BIFF coaching to make yourself look good. Instead, use it to be encouraging to friends, family and/or clients; to reinforce your own BIFF writing skills; and to make the world a more peaceful place.

CHAPTER ELEVEN

You Decide...

You can decide how you will respond to high-conflict people. By now you should realize that you also may decide *how they respond to you!*

Talking to the "Right" Brain

As mentioned in Chapter Three, recent brain research supports the theory of this book – that we have two different methods of conflict resolution, loosely based on the right and left hemispheres of our brains: Logical problem-solving (generally in the left brain) and fast defensive reacting (generally in the right brain). The goal of this book is to help you avoid unnecessarily triggering an HCP's extreme defensiveness, by being Brief, Informative, Friendly and Firm.

A brief summary of these brain dynamics may help you visually remember how to effectively use BIFF responses. Remember that HCPs seem to have a harder time navigating between these two methods because of lack of skills and/or other limitations. They tend to easily slip out of logical problem-solving into fast defensive reacting and, once they are in fast defensive reacting, they have a harder time moving back to logical problem-solving. This is highly influenced by what is happening in the environment, so that anyone will slip into fast defensive reacting if the situation seems threatening enough.

LOGICAL PROBLEM-SOLVING	FAST DEFENSIVE REACTING
• Flexible thinking	• All-or-nothing solutions
• Sees situation as a problem to solve	• Sees situation as an extreme crisis
• Sees necessity for a good analysis	• Sees survival as requiring fast action, not analysis
• Sees the problem as complex, involving bad behaviors	• Sees the problem as bad people
• Sees self as open to improvement	• Sees self as all good (you have to in a crisis)
• Balances problems in context of other issues	• Deals with problems in isolation from other issues
• Sees compromise as normal part of life	• Sees compromise as life-threatening
• Fear and anger can be managed and should not interfere with making good decisions	• Fear and anger are overwhelming and can only be relieved by reacting quickly and defensively

Most of the time the left brain is dominant, but during times of crisis or a very new experience the right brain is dominant. We are living in rapidly changing times of many new experiences. High-conflict people seem to have a lot of difficulty managing change – perhaps because they get more easily stuck in fast defensive reacting. You need to talk to the right brain in the right way, so that the person can calm down and relax. Then, you can talk to the person's left brain about problem-solving.

Managing Your Own Danger Signals

With these differences in mind, the way you respond to high-conflict people – or anyone who is highly upset – can nudge them into one "frame of mind" or the other. While most people can overcome their initial upset emotions and can ignore a momentary negative comment, HCP's become highly defensive and stay stuck there. They are not "reasonable" and can't do logical problem-solving at those times.

With this in mind, you have a choice with many high-conflict people: focus their attention on upsetting emotions (right brain defensiveness), or focus their attention on problem-solving (left brain logical analysis). With good BIFF responses, it appears that you may be able to shift an HCP's attention away from their own unmanageable emotions and actions, and onto reasonable thinking and behavior. However, you usually need to do this quickly. Don't delay or avoid responding – unless no response would be the best. When responding, keep it:

Brief: By keeping it brief, there is less potentially negative information to trigger the HCP's (or anyone's) defensiveness. Even HCPs can handle a tiny bit of potentially negative information, but if it goes on too long they have increasing difficulty staying out of their right-brain defensiveness – and get angry and get stuck.

Informative: This seems to direct their minds to the analytical, left brain problem-solving approach. That's why it's so important to keep this information strictly neutral, rather than judgmental, negative, or disrespectful.

Friendly: When an HCP feels threatened, he or she shifts into all-or-nothing thinking and is unlikely to think logically about the person who appears threatening. However, if an HCP seems stuck in their right hemisphere, being friendly can calm the person down and you may be able to move them back into their left brain. The combination of being friendly and informative seems to help them shift in ways they can't do themselves sometimes.

Firm: If an HCP feels respected, calm and focused on neutral information, then they can let go of most conflicts and get to their calm left hemisphere again. By helping an HCP end a negative or Blamespeak conversation (by email or otherwise), they can relax and no longer feel like they have to defend themselves, so they no longer need to attack you. Since stopping their aggressive behavior is usually the goal, you can help that happen by letting them know you are friendly and done with the conversation. If there is a requested action, then you can end with that – as long as you do it in a brief and friendly manner.

Turning Off Blamespeak in Your Life

Another message of this book is to encourage you to decide to avoid absorbing Blamespeak in your own life, as this can increase your own level of anxiety and make you more vulnerable to slipping into fast defensive reacting without even realizing it. What you hear on the radio, see on television and respond to on the Internet will all shape how you think, to some extent, and what mood you are in.

Ideally, what you hear from the people around you should be positive and logical information as much as possible. Of course, there's no avoiding some negativity, but emphasizing the positive in your relationships will influence how you feel. Feelings are contagious! Blamespeak is particularly contagious, because it is so alarming to your amygdala and can shut down your own logical thinking without even realizing it.

Coaching Others with their BIFF Responses

Now that you can manage your own responses, you may be asked from time to time to review someone else's BIFF response and to coach them on it. You can share all of these same principles with them, but don't overwhelm them with information. When you're a BIFF response coach, you're not a counselor or a lawyer. There's no need to get deep into someone else's situation nor to feel responsible for that person's response. Remember to simply use the 10 Questions and avoid saying too much. In other words, when you're giving your feedback, keep it Brief, Informative, Friendly and Firm. Just keep reminding the person: *"It's up to you. You're the BIFF writer and it's your situation."*

Conclusion

Since HCPs have a harder time managing their upset emotions and shifting over to problem-solving when they are upset, you can do yourself a favor and do it for them. Trying to appear strong and powerful may make you feel good, but it is a trigger for HCP's, who are easily defensive. Instead, try to focus on being non-threatening and reasonable by using BIFF responses. You may decide what they think about by your response.

In closing, I hope I practiced what I preached in this little book. I tried to keep it brief. I attempted to make it informative about what to do, not just why it seems to work. And I hope I was friendly while I was firm. Use BIFF responses and your life should be easier. Period.

Best Wishes!

REFERENCES

6 **Personality disorders:** American Psychiatric Association. (2000). Diagnostic and Statistical Manual of Mental Disorders (4th ed.). Washington, DC.

7-8 **A recent study:** This study was performed with funding by the National Institutes of Health and reported in three separate articles:

NIH study, regarding Narcissistic: Stinson, R. S., Dawson, D. A., Goldstein, R. B. Chou, S. P., Huang, B., Smith, S. M. (2008). Prevalence, correlates, disability, and comorbidity of DSM-IV Narcissistic Personality Disorder: Results from the Wave 2 National Epidemiologic Survey on Alcohol and Related Conditions. *Journal of Clinical Psychiatry, 69*, 1033-1045.

NIH study, regarding Borderline: Grant, B. F., Chou, S. P., Goldstein, R. B., Huang, B., Stinson, F. S., Saha, T. D. (2008). Prevalence, correlates, disability and comorbidity of DSM-IV Borderline Personality disorder: Results from the Wave 2 national epidemiologic survey on alcohol and related conditions. *Journal of Clinical Psychiatry, 69*, 533-545.

NIH study, regarding Paranoid, Antisocial and Histrionic: Grant, B. F., Hasin, D. S., Stinson, R. S.,

Dawson, D. A., Chou, S. P., Ruan, W. J. (2004). Prevalence, correlates, and disability of personality disorders in the United States: Results from the National Epidemiologic Survey on Alcohol and Related Conditions. *Journal of Clinical Psychiatry, 65,* 948-958.

37   **Our brains are mostly divided:** The information about the differences of the right and left hemispheres of the brain has been drawn from several books, including:

Schore, A. N. (2003). *Affect Regulation and the Repair of the Self.* New York, NY: W. W. Norton & Company.

Goldberg, E. (2005). *The Wisdom Paradox: How Your Mind Can Grow Stronger As Your Brain Grows Older.* New York, NY: Gotham Books.

Seigel, D. J. (1999). *The Developing Mind: How Relationships and the Brain Interact to Shape Who We Are.* New York, NY: The Guilford Press.

Seigel, D. J. (2007). *The Mindful Brain: Reflection and Attunement in the Cultivation of Well-Being.* New York, NY: W. W. Norton & Company.

38   **The amygdala acts like a smoke alarm:** Goleman, D. (2006). *Social Intelligence: The New Science of Human Relationships.* New York, NY: Bantam Dell.

39   **Most of the time, the left brain is dominant:** Schore at 270.

39   **Much of this wisdom seems to be stored in the left:** Goldberg at 195-205.

40   **Brain scientists have learned that you can change your own brain:** Doidge, N. (2007). *The Brain that Changes Itself: Stories of Personal Triumph from the Frontiers of Brain Science.* New York, NY: Penguin Books.

123-124   **Public relations quote:** Doyle, P. (2009). *Domino's President Responds to Prank Video.* April 18, 2009. From http://www.youtube.com/watch?v=dem6eA7-A2I.

125   **Brain research has shown that emotions are contagious:** Iacoboni, M. (2008). *Mirroring People: The New Science of How We Connect with Others.* New York, NY: Farrar, Straus and Giroux.

145   **"false and misleading statements:"** Kern, J. (2007). *Aguirre vs. Sanders.* San Diego Union-Tribune, October 14, 2007, G-1, 5.

145   **$3.5 million:** Nelson, D. (2007). *The Uncivil War at City Hall.* San Diego Magazine, October, 2007, 17.

145   **"And while people say:** Kern at G5.

149   **"one of the most corrupt:** MCT News Service, *Issa to Take Aim at Spending.* San Diego Union-Tribune, January 3, 2011, A-7.

WILLIAM A. ("BILL") EDDY is president of High Conflict Institute, based in San Diego, California. He is a Certified Family Law Specialist in California with over twenty years' experience representing clients in family court and providing divorce mediation out of court. Prior to becoming a lawyer, he worked as a Licensed Clinical Social Worker with twelve years' experience providing therapy to children, adults, couples and families in psychiatric hospitals and outpatient clinics.

As president and co-founder of High Conflict Institute, Bill has become an international speaker on the subject of high-conflict personalities to attorneys, judges, mediators, therapists, human resource, EAP and collaborative professionals, in over twenty-five states, Canada, France, Sweden, Australia and New Zealand. High Conflict Institute is dedicated to providing training, resources and program development to professionals dealing with high-conflict personalities in legal disputes, workplace disputes, healthcare disputes, and education disputes. The New Ways for Families™ program was developed by Bill in 2009 for the High Conflict Institute as an intervention method for potentially high-conflict families in family courts. His New Ways for Mediation™ method was developed in 2013 to provide more structure and skills for potentially high-conflict clients of any type of mediation.

He is part-time faculty of the National Judicial College, providing training to state and federal judges in handling high-conflict people in court, and is also part-time faculty of the Strauss Institute for Dispute Resolution at the School of Law at Pepperdine University. He serves as the Senior Family Mediator at the National Conflict Resolution Center in San Diego, California, and has taught Negotiation and Mediation for six years at the University of San Diego School of Law.

Bill obtained his law degree in 1992 from the University of San Diego, a Master of Social Work degree in 1981 from San Diego State University, and a Bachelor's degree in Psychology in 1970 from Case Western Reserve University. He began his career as a youth social worker in a changing neighborhood in New York City. He considers conflict resolution the theme of his varied career.

If you would like to send an email about your experiences, what you've learned from this book, or anything else, please contact Bill at info@highconflictinstitute.com You can read Bill's blog at http://highconflictinstitute.com/blog/

For help with BIFF, visit www.biffresponse.com

— II —